MARIJUANA WITHDRAWAL AFTER 40 YEARS

60-Days of a Withdrawal Odyssey

Leo A. Sielsch

Book Publishers Network

Book Publishers Network
P.O. Box 2256
Bothell • WA • 98041
Ph • 425-483-3040
www.bookpublishersnetwork.com

Copyright © 2011 by Leo A. Sielsch
Chapter graphic © Aleksejs Kostins | Dreamstime.com

All rights reserved. No part of this book may be reproduced, stored in, or introduced into a retrieval system, or transmitted in any form, or by any means (electronic, mechanical, photocopying, recording, or otherwise) without the prior written permission of the publisher.

10 9 8 7 6 5 4 3 2 1

Printed in the United States of America

    LCCN 2011904806
    ISBN10 1-935359-78-9
    ISBN13 978-1-935359-78-4

Editor: Julie Scandora
Cover designer: Laura Zugzda

CONTENTS

PREFACE v
  DAY 1: WHY WITHDRAW? 1
  DAY 2: WHY SMOKE SHIT? 3
  DAY 3: WEIGHT CONTROL? 5
  DAY 4: MUSIC LISTENING? 9
  DAY 5: NEWSPAPER FREAK 11
  DAY 6: WHAT ABOUT SEX? 13
  DAY 7: ABOUT THE BELL 15
  DAY 8: REMEMBER ALZHEIMER'S 17
  DAY 9: STOCK MARKET STRESS 19
  DAY 10: STOCK MARKET RELIEF 21
  DAY 11: NERO WOLFE 23
  DAY 12: RESTLESS LEG SYNDROME 25
  DAY 13: REST DAY 29
  DAY 14: THE MUNCHIES 31
  DAY 15: PSYCHOLOGICAL TEST 33
  DAY 16: ELEMENTS OF JAZZ 35
  DAY 17: 401K INVESTMENT 37
  DAY 18: HOME-GROWN 41
  DAY 19: GOOD OLD DAYS 43
  DAY 20: ECONOMICS CONSIDERED 47
  DAY 21: PLEASURE/PAIN PRINCIPLE 49
  DAY 22: EQUIPMENT USAGE 51
  DAY 23: HODGEPODGE 57
  DAY 24: STOCK MARKET 59
  DAY 25: MEMORY PROBLEMS 63
  DAY 26: PHILOSOPHY 65
  DAY 27: TOOTHBRUSH MACHINES 67

DAY 28: LOVE AND LIFE	69
DAY 29: MODERATION	75
DAY 30: POT LOOK-ALIKES	77
DAY 31: WITHDRAW AND PREPARATION	79
DAY 32: JOY CHANGES	81
DAY 33: SEPTUAGENARIAN SEX	87
DAY 34: TIGER GOLF	95
DAY 35: LEGALIZATION	97
DAY 36: HODGEPODGE	101
DAY 37: CHILDHOOD FACTOR	103
DAY 38: PINBALL TILT	109
DAY 39: ALCOHOL	115
DAY 40: HODGEPODGE	119
DAY 41: PATIENCE	121
DAY 42: TV WEED	123
DAY 43: HODGEPODGE	129
DAY 44: EYE EXAMS	131
DAY 45: ADDICTION	133
DAY 46: WEEDS AND FAMILY	137
DAY 47: BUYING SHIT	143
DAY 48: WIKIPEDIA	147
DAY 49: CONFIDENCE	151
DAY 50: END DECISION	155
DAY 51: WIFE OF MY LIFE	159
DAY 52: THE CHURCH	169
DAY 53: WHY GOD?	171
DAY 54: MEDICATION TRIAL	173
DAY 58: TEST RUN	175
DAY 60: FINAL ANALYSIS	177
CONCLUSION	179
ADDENDUM: MEDICAL MARIJUANA	181

PREFACE

Why would I want to withdraw from my pleasurable daily use of marijuana? Even more, why would I want to write about my habit and expose it to the world with the federal government still rejecting marijuana's legalization and general use? Why would I reveal my long-held secret use of pot? Will these revelations negatively affect my family?

I needed a crutch! I needed a motivator! I needed a daily pressure to keep me from losing my resolve and having a hit. You are now reading my withdrawal assistant that provided the major mind-control energy required to make my withdrawal happen.

I am in good health. I am not suffering from any health problem. But I do have concerns about my long-term indulgence. Let's face it, inhaling a drug for forty years made me wonder. Most of all, I sensed a memory problem that I felt was an early warning of Alzheimer's disease. So I devised a way to determine if my using marijuana or not using it was contributing to how well I remember. And this withdrawal journal shows the results of that test.

In addition, before and after I started my diary, I was continually searching the Web for reliable data related to marijuana. Although anecdotes were easily found on both sides of the health and legalization issues, I found almost no creditable test results of the positive or negative use of pot. The lack of testing, especially of long-term use, was part of my motivation for engaging in this withdrawal experiment. By providing information about the state of my health in relation to marijuana, I hope to help those using as well as those anticipating using this drug.

The other aspect of my research and writing involved addressing the questions that arise around canceling the prohibition of marijuana and legislating a set of usage conditions. The media has given significant coverage of this issue with various government, education, and law enforcement officials speaking out on the subject but has found no consensus on what action, if any, to take. Medical marijuana usage is presently active in fourteen states with others studying and thinking of enacting similar legislation. The debate continues, and in this journal, I contribute my own opinions, based on my observations, others' findings, and personal experience.

Throughout the recordings of my sixty-day experiment, I kept an open mind, constantly asking what results I was getting, to determine the effects of marijuana usage on my life—physical, mental, and emotional—now and in the future. I sincerely hope you will benefit from my work.

Finally, I believe my publishing team did an excellent job of organizing and editing my work, and I thank them.

DAY 1: WHY WITHDRAW?

The writing of this book is this addict's choice of assistance to achieve, hopefully, a long-term abstinence of daily marijuana usage. This habit of mine is now forty years old, and there are no indications of major health problems at the present time. The object of my attempt at abstinence is to assess the present pleasures of daily usage and weigh the potential risks of continuing the habit.

I was a pack-a-day cigarette smoker starting at age seventeen during the years when cigarette smoking was not considered an unhealthy activity. More people smoked than didn't smoke. Although there were filter cigarettes available (but not very popular), I chose the non-filter type. Eventually, evidence indicating the dangers of cig smoking began to appear in various newspapers, magazines, and other sources.

I was successful in curbing my cigarette habit at age forty-eight, resulting in sixteen years of abstinence. Unfortunately, I relapsed after my retirement but maintained a much lesser usage, often smoking only a couple of cigs in a day. But some days were bad, and I might smoke up to a pack a day. This reduction of cigarette smoking made it difficult to abstain totally, even though the evidence of potential health problems was everywhere. I was now in my seventies and was frequently coughing up phlegm. When I decided to leave California to move to the state of Washington, I felt this change could be a good time to quit cigarettes forever. And I did!

And now I wonder about my other smoking habit. As I write this intro, I have not smoked my shit for one day. Will I be able to abstain for the two months' goal that I have resolved to accomplish? That is the question. If you are reading this "DAY 1" from my book, then you know I succeeded!

DAY 2: WHY SMOKE SHIT?

I am not having any difficulty without the weed, but that is what is written about withdrawal, no pain or bodily discomfort.

The question that many people ask is: why do you smoke marijuana? I have a very simple answer, which applies to most people involved with drugs. It makes me feel better after I smoke than I did before I smoked. But my habit had another strong effect that became my main desire to smoke.

I was, am, and probably always will be a person who believes that no day should go by without learning something. All my life, I have been a serious learner. And how did this preoccupation with my continually striving to improve my knowledge and skills affect my personal relationships?

It had abominable repercussions. Don't talk to me about your social activities, your everyday experiences, your entertainment pleasantries. You will sense the discomfort I feel, and eventually, you won't even attempt to have day-to-day conversations with me.

Guess what? The high that I received from my weed habit not only made me feel good. It also relaxed me to the extent that I could be a social being. I laughed, I listened, I participated in social intercourse and actually enjoyed myself. And so did others about me.

I always controlled my dope habit. I never indulged myself either in the workplace or before going to the workplace. This was not a difficult task because, as I stated before, there are no bothersome withdrawal sensations, thus making it a somewhat simple practice to resist using at the times I found it important to do so. I was still looking forward to having a toke for it did then, as it does now, make me feel relaxed and a happy smoker.

All those years that I was a user, I thought about the problems this habit could cause in my throat or my lungs. I always felt that cigarettes were even worse. But somehow, pleasure is powerful, and you find a way to rationalize your habit.

DAY 3: WEIGHT CONTROL?

I am not having any difficulty without the weed. The difficulty I have had over the years has been getting good shit without risking my life and costing me an arm and a leg. I suspect that over the forty-some years of use, I have spent over eighty thousand dollars, or an average of two hundred dollars per month. Since I moved to the state of Washington in 2007, I have had a very steady and reliable source of good quality stuff.

When I reflect on the various so-called dealers and situations that I found myself in when making a buy, I am so happy to have had the last four good years. During my life as an addict, I probably have made purchases from thirty different people, male and female, young and old. Have I been ripped off? Yes, but not often. If I made a purchase and it turned out to be junk, I would buy no more from that dealer.

I mentioned earlier that I was a cigarette smoker starting at age seventeen when I graduated from high school. From that time until I was thirty years of age, I smoked brands such as Lucky Strike—LSMFT, or Lucky Strike Means Fine Tobacco, I believe was the saying. I also smoked Pall Mall, Camel, Chesterfield, etc., all non-filters. So what happened at age thirty? Well, I found Sherman, a cigarette that was rolled in a tobacco housing instead of white paper. I felt that many of the potential health problems with cigarettes may not be the tobacco but rather the paper it is rolled into. So the majority of my cigarette years, I smoked the paperless Sherman that also advertised its omission of saltpeter, which is present in most cigarette brands. As stated earlier, I did successfully quit for a period of sixteen years, age forty-seven to age sixty-three. Although I did return to cig smoking again when I retired, I never returned to the pack-a-day routine. In fact, there were many days when I smoked not one cigarette. Eventually, I quit altogether. Was it difficult to quit? Yes. But moving to another state was helpful. Also I was producing phlegm (one of the toughest words to spell) too often, and it was frightening in addition to being just plain nasty. Four years later, after quitting, I do not have a problem with phlegm even though I smoked my weed every day.

It is interesting to tell you that the two types of smoking, weed and cigs, were definitely factors in my body weight. Cigarettes suppressed my appetite, and grass enhanced it. I found that when I smoked a lot of marijuana, I had a difficult time restraining my appetite, and I needed to do a lot of walking to offset or burn off those calories consumed. The munchies, as the pangs of hunger are called, were an ever-present temptation and required much policing and special control to avoid becoming overweight. The challenge of keeping my weight at a certain level intensified when I could no longer carry out my favorite hobby, walking. During my years after fifty, I walked an average of thirty miles a week. This was in addition to my walking on the golf course, carrying my bag, at least twice a week. In my opinion, this exercise and the scarcity of bad food items in my kitchen have kept me healthy—at least until recently.

But what happens now that my right knee, which I seriously injured at age fourteen, has finally given out and I can walk only a few blocks before having great pain? Do I pay now for the mistakes of my youth?

I was a very active athletic youngster, but also a stupid one. I was thirteen, and I was playing Tarzan, climbing a tree and yelling as he did in the movies. I was about fifteen feet up in the tree, and I decided to emulate Tarzan by leaping to another branch, which was a few feet away. I jumped and easily reached the branch except there was one problem that I hadn't thought about. The branch was thick, I would say about five inches in diameter. As I swung and landed on the branch, the centrifugal force of my leap caused my hands to rotate about the branch to the point where I could not maintain my grip. Down I went! My right ankle was hurting badly.

There I was, lying on the ground in great pain. The other guys went and brought my father who supported me while I hobbled on my left foot. We headed to a doctor who was less than a block away. Fortunately, the doctor was immediately available to examine my foot. I had a fractured ankle, he decided without taking any X-rays, just from his hands moving the ankle and my screaming. He taped the ankle and told my father that I would need crutches and would need to use them for about six to eight weeks. So no more tree-climbing for me.

Something else was damaged in that fall, something that I didn't realize for many years, unfortunately, something that also should have been cared for soon after the accident. Apparently, the force of hitting the hard dirt ground, which caused my fractured ankle, also stretched one of the ligaments that keeps the upper part of the knee held firmly to the lower part. At the time, and even thereafter, I felt no pain from this strained ligament. My ankle eventually healed, and I got off the crutches, and life for me returned to normal. Or so I thought. One year later, I visited with my grandparents at a wonderful place at the New Jersey shore. My friends and I were on the beach, swimming, running, and playing. I had a blanket, and on that day, when we were ready to leave, I bent down to pick up the blanket. As I rose, I felt a resistance as I was about halfway up. My knee did not want to straighten up. So I forced it. I overcame the resistance, having no understanding of what was going on. As I straightened out my leg, I heard this loud "pop" and suddenly had great pain in my knee. Apparently, the strained ligament did not securely hold my knee structure the way it was supposed to. The knee was partially out of the socket, no longer centered as it should have been. The pop that I heard was the offset knee bone crushing the knee cartilage, and apparently, the pop was the cartilage partially forced out of its proper central cushioning position in the knee joint. It was painful, but I soon got my knee back to its correct structural relationship. I was able to walk though it was painful. What I didn't realize was that I had displaced some of that absorbent cartilage.

This uneven cartilage, accompanied by the strained and stretched ligament, allowed my knee to come out of its socket. Certain movements would result in this problem, which was now compounded because of the cartilage displacement that occurred on the beach. But when this happened, I was aware, and before I vigorously straightened my leg I was careful to allow the knee joint to achieve a proper alignment before straightening my leg. This reaction of the knee parts to movements in a particular direction changed my life. I could no longer participate in any sport that required a turning motion that could cause the misalignment. It didn't take too many hurts caused by this condition to make me realize which sporting activities I had to abandon. And each time I got into that awkward position, I knew that I had to carefully align my knee prior to straightening it. Each time this occurred, it would take a couple of days before I could walk properly with no pain. The result was no tennis; basketball; baseball; football; or any activity with a potential to cause me that problem. So much for my active sports life. Fortunately, bowling did not give me a problem, and that became my sport for a number of years. I also began to play golf, with knee braces at times, but I could play. My swing was not conventional, but I could play.

DAY 4: MUSIC LISTENING?

No problems on this fourth day. No withdrawal aches, resulting in another good day of abstinence. Have I lost weight because of these days without excessive appetite? No, but I feel I am eating normally and expect that over time this behavior will enable me to reach my desired weight of 154. Presently I am at 165.

What changes in my appreciation and joy of music have occurred? So far very little. My joy in listening to music has been—and continues to be—a major pleasure during my lifetime.

During my twenties, in the late fifties and early sixties, many fine restaurants featured live music. Quite often, a trio on the piano, bass, and drums entertained the customers, of which I was one, and I really enjoyed the good sounds. However, it seems to me when I think back, many fine eateries discontinued this practice. They either dropped it completely or provided a single piano player.

Although I miss hearing those instruments in restaurants, I have other means to enjoy music, thanks to modern technology. In fact, just today I purchased a jazz trio album from Amazon.com. Because of the tremendous improvements in both the availability of music for listening before buying and the new marvelous and inexpensive music players and headphones, I initiated a special musical project as part of this experiment in withdrawing from marijuana. The smoking of weed plus using the wonderful headphones of today and having the unbelievable selection of music songs available have sweetened my pleasure of music listening over the years. The thought of removing any of those three was bothersome, and in this two-month test, would I find the pleasing and sensitive sounds of listening less joyful without marijuana?

DAY 5: NEWSPAPER FREAK

To me, a newspaper freak, Friday is a special day. I presently have two papers daily, the *Seattle Times* and *USA Today*. Every morning I arise between two thirty and three in the morning. I would like to sleep longer, but five hours is about as much sleep as I ever get. I go to bed between nine and eleven in the evening because I am tired. But I don't mind getting up early because the papers (during the week) arrive somewhere around two thirty. Every morning I get some mental exercise by doing the Jumble, Sudoku, and crossword puzzles in both papers. I believe mental exercise is just as important as physical exercise, and I make the two part of my routine. I go to Bally's every morning at six forty-five and return at eight. I have been doing both the mental and physical exercises for the past four years since I moved to Washington State.

I don't know how familiar you are with the crossword and Sudoku puzzles, but they start out very simple and easy on Mondays but get harder each successive day of the week. Friday is a special day. Why? Because the puzzles are tough. Especially the Sudoku. I cut the puzzles from the newspapers and take them to my printer. There I make two enlarged copies and can't wait to tackle them. It's interesting to me, and maybe others, how the order in selecting and reading the contents of the newspapers has changed over the years. For many years the sports page was my opening selection. That has changed drastically. Now it is puzzles first, followed by the business section. (I am involved in the stock market, which opens at 6:30 a.m. Pacific time. More about this activity coming up later.)

Now the reason I make copies of the Sudoku is that, on Fridays, they are rated five stars, meaning they are tough as hell. I find myself often making errors and needing to print extra copies to try again. But today, day five of my abstinence, I was practically able to run through the solving process and finished both puzzles the first try in almost record time. I don't know if it was just a coincidence that I was so successful at completing the Sudokus. That is, did my abstinence—remember this is day five—make my brain work better, or was something else at work? After all, I have had other Fridays where I got good results, but not very often both puzzles like today. It will take more than this one incident to convince me that avoiding smoking the weed caused me to perform Sudoku so well. But it is something that I will watch in the future.

DAY 6: WHAT ABOUT SEX?

Feeling good, I thought I might write a few words about marijuana and sex. Once I became a marijuana user, I never had sex again without it. Why? First of all because it seemed to feel better being loaded than not. Whenever I was with the woman of that time and we were fooling around, romancing, I believed that if I were under the influence I was more apt to jump into the sack with my lover. Not all of the women in my life after I became a user were also users. I did not mind if they were not high as I was, as long as they didn't object to my weed smoking.

    Well, what did this habit do for me in the bedroom? It released me from some of the normal inhibitions I experienced during my pre-use days. It seemed to extend my climax from seconds to minutes. I am sure that was just my perception, but it didn't matter if that was true or not. It was what I felt. Unfortunately or not, I finally find, at my present age, that my interest for sexual activity has diminished whether I smoke or not. Probably a major factor in this decline was the lack of a participating partner. I am not complaining; in fact, I am somewhat relieved for my drive to the bedroom was strong over the years, especially my younger years, and often got me into difficult situations. I have a lot more to say about my lifetime sexual joys and failures.

DAY 7: ABOUT THE BELL

Today is the last day of my first week without my weed. I am writing this at one forty-five in the morning because I am having trouble sleeping. So while I was lying in bed, I was listening with my headphones to music, noticing a slight difference without my stuff. But it was still fine. Then I got to thinking about my hearing. It is not the greatest at this age, and although it hasn't been really good for over twenty years, I don't blame its weakening on my drug habit. But it got me thinking.

I don't know if you remember the figure of the bell, used to show the distribution of the population's IQ (intelligence quotient) scores. A book, *The Bell Curve—Intelligence and Class Structure in American Life*, written by Richard Herrnstein and Charles Murray, placed IQ scores along one side of a graph and percent levels along the other side. For each IQ score, they indicated the percent of the population that had scored at that level. The distribution of the scores took on the shape of a bell. Deep on the left side of the bell, where it was low, indicating a small percent, were those born with a low IQ; deep on the right side, equally low and also indicating a small percent of the population, were those born with a high IQ; and the large central portion, the main part of the bell, indicating the high percent of the population, was the average IQ. I wasn't thinking about IQ this evening but thought of my application, over the years, of using the bell curve for listing the levels of human hearing, sight, height, etc., similar to our IQ measurements. Yes, we could use this same bell shape to describe data related to a population's physical height. Just substitute height measurements for IQ scores, and you will have a similar shape—with a few people with short stature on the deep left side of the bell, a few very tall individuals on the deep right-hand side, and most people, who are of average height, in the middle.

Why am I writing about the bell curve in this book? Because I believe that every person has different levels of ability with his or her senses. These differences can affect your life in many different manners. Take me and my sense of hearing. If a professional measured my hearing abilities and placed the results on a graph with poor hearing on the left increasing to extremely sensitive hearing on the far right, you would find my results deep on the left side. This doesn't mean I can't hear, but I have problems with noisy environments, such as parties, restaurants, and even listening to TV. I am sure that with aging one's hearing capabilities deteriorate.

But it is not hearing that affects the writing of this book. Memory applies both to the power of remembering and to what is remembered. Memory has a number of synonyms that apply to the various aspects of what has been learned or experienced in one's past. Remembrance applies to the act of remembering while recollection adds an implication of consciously bringing back to mind with some effort. Finally, reminiscence generally refers to pleasant experiences from a remote past.

I utilize all of the above in writing this diary. The reason I bring the bell curve into this explanation is that, if my memory abilities could be measured, I am sure that I would find my score on the deep left part of the bell. In other words, I started out with a poor memory. I remember (yes I do) I had great problems in high school on testing that required good recollections of learned material. For me, trigonometry was the ball-buster. I never could remember the formulas and other material necessary to do well in the trig tests, and I never got decent grades in that course. However, I was a whiz in algebra where memory played a much smaller part and logical thinking was the key.

I mention this because during these writing efforts I found myself working hard to recollect experiences from forty, fifty, or more years ago. I found myself using every technique I could think of to stimulate my brain to recall experiences that I remembered but not well.

DAY 8: REMEMBER ALZHEIMER'S

If I thought that not indulging myself with Mary Jane my strong appetite for munchies would vanish, I was totally wrong. I still have a strong desire for goodies. I certainly hope that as my abstinence continues my munchies will discontinue, although I have my doubts.

I just printed a ten-page report on marijuana addiction published by drug-rehab at the site drug.rehab.com/marijuana-addiction.htm. I intend to assess carefully the information contained in this report and report and compare my feelings and findings during this abstinence activity. It states, and I agree, cannabinoid receptors in the brain influence pleasure, memory, thought, concentration, sensory and time perception, and coordinated movement. The question is: does it affect the smoker negatively only in the short term or does it have more long-lasting effects?

This introduces the possibility that memory problems could, for long-time addicts such as myself, be heading toward Alzheimer's disease. The connection between marijuana and such extreme memory loss would be somewhat difficult to assess because there are millions of people who contract Alzheimer's that never have smoked marijuana!

I never felt any lessening of my ability to do puzzles, such as crosswords, or solve computer complexities. I do admit that I presently am not as sharp as I was twenty years ago, but you show me someone who is nearly eighty and hasn't weakened some in his or her problem-solving abilities.

I am not trying to convince anyone that smoking marijuana is a healthy hobby. There are many habits we acquire in our lifetime that are not good for us. But we do them. We do them even knowing the mostly negative health warnings, such as contained in the report I just printed. Would I have had a better life had I never smoked grass? What is a "better" life? We establish a life philosophy over time that has a strong influence on our interests and behavior, especially in our declining years. I never was exposed to the drug until I was thirty-five years old. That, for sure, is a factor in its effect on my body and brain that may differ from one who gets started at age seventeen.

I also believe that levels of usage counts; indulging all day, only in the evening, or only on weekends all could result in different responses by the body and brain. To me, it is the same as a person having an eating situation and overeating sugar foods to the point of becoming obese. People who eat the same sugary items but in much smaller quantities will generally do so without negative results. Moderation! But can an addict limit his pleasures to the level that is somewhat safe?

Until this year of 2010, most information about the effects of marijuana on a smoker's Alzheimer's disease were negative. Some scientists even concluded that smoking marijuana would help to protect grass smokers from the memory problems of Alzheimer's disease. However, a newly developed brain-imaging method allows physicians to diagnose Alzheimer's before its onset. Building upon a recent discovery that the same Alzheimer's disease process that goes on in the brain also occurs in the eye, researchers have developed a pair of optical tests that can determine the presence of amyloid beta proteins—found in all Alzheimer's patients—in the lens of the eye. A device called an interior laser ophthalmoscope can pick up the presence of the amyloid protein.

A new study, using mice carrying human genetic mutations that cause Alzheimer's disease, gave them doses of HU210—also known as cannabinoids—and they did no better than the untreated mice. The study showed that HU210 has no biological or behavioral effect on the established Alzheimer's model. More studies are required before much hope in the use of marijuana to prevent Alzheimer's disease can be proven.

DAY 9: STOCK MARKET STRESS

I was hoping that removing weed from my daily usage might, in some way, improve my sleeping habits. It isn't that I have had trouble sleeping because I do sleep well. Most important, it takes only a few minutes for me to fall soundly asleep. The problem was I could sleep for only about five hours, and so far into the ninth day of this test, I still cannot sleep more than five hours. I do not want to use any over-the-counter or prescribed sleeping pills, although the info I find on the Web suggests that one should sleep seven to eight hours.

The time of day does not show on these writings, but I will tell you that many of them are written between the hours of three and five in the morning. What other activities do I engage in during those early morning hours? I spend a lot of time researching stock market information. Because of the low interest rates (less than .5 percent) in my IRA CDs, I rolled my accounts over to a stock market account with Scottrade. My attempt to maintain or increase the value of my account (eventually to be left to my children) has, unfortunately, not worked out as I anticipated. I got off to a great start, increasing the value by 10 percent in the first eight months. However, this improvement is gone. The market has become very volatile, and as of today, my account has been reduced from my original rollover amount by 10 percent. And I think that it will get worse before it improves. I have been especially hit hard because I chose to invest in lo-cap bio-health stocks, which have been hit the hardest of all sectors.

DAY 10: STOCK MARKET RELIEF

There is no doubt that stressful situations can break your resolutions, whatever they may be. It is especially true for me even though I really do not have any major problems. However, in the last two months I have had losses in my stock portfolio. And I can't get out of the market at this time without taking a major loss. Why am I involved with the stock market? For the last couple of years, I put my resources into a CD that paid at least 5 percent. This investment created enough earnings to satisfy my yearly minimum distribution amount without eroding the principal. Unfortunately, the interest rate during the recession dropped to 0.5 percent or less, which meant that my yearly distribution cut into and greatly reduced my principal. The money markets were just as sad, and I felt that gold was not the answer. However, now looking back, rolling my IRA over to gold would have been a wise move. But I felt the stock market was at a very low level and that the government's efforts to avoid catastrophe in the financial, housing, and overall economic situations would present many good opportunities. This resulted in unrealized earnings of about ten thousand dollars in 2009. And I was very happy with the initial returns—until April, May, and June of 2010.

These losses were not causing me any daily financial problems. After all, the losses were unrealized, but I knew that the current market conditions would make it very difficult to make up these recent losses, and that realization gave me stress. Normally, if I was not abstaining from pot usage, I would have definitely increased my intake, intending to let it help me feel less serious and upset. I must admit that yesterday and today I did feel some urges to have a hit or two. But I didn't.

Having a hit would not improve my present stock portfolio, but it would lessen my concerns about it. It is way too soon even to begin to think about relapsing. It would erase all of the efforts I have made to curtail my addiction up to this point. Although this point is only ten days, it is not nearly enough abstinence to learn anything about the long-term effects of smoking marijuana.

DAY 11: NERO WOLFE

It is now four thirty in the morning. When I awake and before I rise from my bed in the morning, usually starting at about two thirty, I think about what am I going to write today. Well the theme for my early words today is: where did all the laughter go? Probably the most powerful reaction that I experienced in my early days of smoking joints was a great deal of laughter. At this time of my life, I was living with Barbara, a young lady who was fifteen years younger than I. I was thirty-five, she was twenty one. We both laughed almost every time we hit on a joint. At that time, I thought that rolling a joint was the way everybody smoked.

Since I was not adept at rolling the joint with my fingers, I soon purchased a roller, in fact more than one. Why? Because there were two sizes.

(There was an interruption while I was typing this page. A computer update took over, and there was nothing I could do but wait it out. I was ready to get angry because I am not a good typist—I never learned how, and I never thought I would need to—and in addition, I was afraid I would lose my thoughts. I told myself they couldn't possibly make these updates without considering what the user is doing. So I waited patiently; in fact, I went to the bathroom and brushed my teeth. That kept me somewhat busy instead of sitting by my Dell and getting upset while I was waiting. At any rate I am back, checked this file to see if I lost anything; thank goodness I didn't. So I saved it, and here I am back at work.)

There are many thoughts that I will express and attempt to explain before I am finished with the story of my abstentious feelings. I must add that probably the most powerful thoughts that were the instigators of my abstinence exercise were related to my poor memory and the possibility of Alzheimer's disease. So you will find that I will probably repeat myself many times in this book. As the pages grow in number, it will take a great deal of searching to ascertain evidence of prior mention of items. Therefore, I am not going to do that search. I am going to write freely and certainly try not to repeat myself. I read somewhere that the author Rex Stout who wrote about seventy-eight novels related to his detective, Nero Wolfe, remembered all the characters, addresses, or other information from previous books he had written.

DAY 12: RESTLESS LEG SYNDROME

The time is 1:12 a.m. I went to bed at 8:15 p.m. very tired. I fell asleep practically as soon as I touched the bed. I knew I would be faced with waking at a very early hour, and here I am. This is one of those moments when it is very tempting to have a good strong hit, which would really help me sleep a few more hours.

I don't remember if I mentioned previously that I suffer from RLS, restless leg syndrome. Where shall I start with this problem? Let's start at the beginning, a time in which I felt the symptoms but never had heard of RLS. It was awful because I had feelings that I truly couldn't describe. I never attempted to explain what I felt to the doctor because it was such a weird feeling. What would I tell him, "Hey, Doc, I've got electricity running up and down my legs"? I felt he would think I was crazy; after all, it wasn't painful. When the feelings occurred during the day, I could relieve them by walking, which I did. I lived on Whitley Terrace, a beautiful street in Hollywood located above Hollywood Boulevard. The main big street nearby was Highland; the Hollywood Bowl was about three blocks away down the hill. The homes in this community were mostly built around the turn of the century, I mean the years between 1900 and 1910. And many movie stars lived here over the years. When I first moved in, Donald O'Conner lived across the street, and Lillian Gish lived up the street. Whitley Terrace, the main street of Whitley Heights, was about eight-tenths of a mile, running in a circle. It was a very wonderful situation for me, a walker at the time. And guess what?

Walking was one of the best ways for me to allay the electricity that I felt in my legs. It usually worked. Sometimes I walked for an hour, sometimes longer. Fortunately, the Sony Walkman was available at that time. I set the station presets to four FM stations that played the music that I enjoyed. I never listened to the commercials. As soon as a commercial began, I would switch the station. Samo samo for any songs that I disliked—onto another station. Normally, this exercise activity would reduce these electric-like feelings I had so that I could return to my normal activities. Bedtime was another story. My legs just couldn't stay still. It was driving me crazy. What would I do to alleviate this shitty feeling, making it almost impossible to sleep? I would arise and smoke a lot of dope; I was hoping to reach a state of stupor strong enough to enable me to sleep. Sometimes I feel that it helped; other times I was up most of the night.

    I had a horrible experience that I didn't know until much later was caused by RLS. The year 1999 was my fiftieth year from graduating high school in Reading, Pennsylvania. I planned to attend the reunion that year. I had attended my fortieth year previously, and it had given me the opportunity to visit the best friend of my youth, Paul Bausch. But this trip was going to be more than my high school reunion. A good friend of mine for many years and a fellow golfer, Bob Hamilton, was planning a European trip to purchase a BMW, drive it in Europe, and then have it shipped back to the USA. He was a representative for a number of manufacturers in Germany, and thus he would meet with them and update his working knowledge of the companies' products and new items. Well, I am not, at this time, going to relate to you my sometimes wonderful, sometimes not experiences on this my first and only trip to Europe.

    What does this trip have to do with today's theme? Well, it concerns the return flight. I may have a bad memory, but I still remember the irritating moments of the airplane ride home. Now remember I had no knowledge of RLS. I had never heard of it, nor did I know that designation was for what I had been feeling. I began to feel the awful, I call it electric, feeling during this flight. Fortunately, I had an aisle seat, which enabled me to get up at least once in a while. But this small amount of walking to the latrine didn't do very much to relieve my ill feelings. So I had to live somehow with it until the flight was over. It was awful. I felt that I was on that plane for days. I am not a religious person, but I prayed we could get there soon. Awful, awful, awful.

I had a dial-up connection to the Internet, which I had initiated sometime before my trip to Europe. It was on one of my excursions on the Web after my return that I ran into the term, restless leg syndrome. I learned, according to the articles I read, that over twelve million people suffer from this illness, its name shortened to RLS. I can tell you that after I learned of this malady I couldn't wait to visit with my Doctor Brousseau at UCLA and describe as best as I could my problem. He was fully aware of RLS. It didn't take him very long to prescribe a medication for me called Mirapex. And best of all, it worked. I was one of those people who disliked taking medication and did everything I could not to take pills. However, this changed because the Mirapex truly relieved my RLS. Hallelujah. Hallelujah.

But ... it always seems when taking medication there is a but! For me it was constipation, which I had rarely experienced. So naturally, I complained to Brousseau about this condition that had aroused from the usage of the Mirapex medication. He told me to handle the problems of constipation since there were no other medications at that time that would relieve the symptoms of RLS, not heal the ailment but provide relief so one could sleep. Needless to say, I have much more to tell you about my handling of the constipation problem, and I will do so in the future.

Today is a Friday, and as I mentioned before, Friday mornings are special to me. My two daily newspapers will be here shortly with their challenging puzzles.

One more thing before I quit for the day. Many times during my taking of Mirapex, I would discontinue it for a short period of time to see if I still had the problem. I did! Now after more time without my dope, I want, again, to experiment with no Mirapex. All of my Google searches on the Web found information that the smoking of grass reduces the irritation of RLS. But during my withdrawal, I will try to get along without my Mirapex and will definitely let you know of the results.

DAY 13: REST DAY

This was a Saturday, another day for difficult Sudokus, one with a six-star difficulty rating in the *Seattle Times* and one in the *Sunday SeattleTtimes*, which I purchase on Saturday even though I will also receive it on Sunday. Just can't wait, and I have plenty of time on Saturday. Exercised as usual, but Bally's doesn't open until eight in the morning on the weekend. Thought more about my noticeable change in behavior during my withdrawal and am determined to be more sensitive in relationship situations.

DAY 14: THE MUNCHIES

F---! I had the munchies this morning. I did not have anything for munching. I was desperate from the early morning till I just had to have something. I already had a sausage and some mango pieces, which should have been enough. But it wasn't. What should I do? It must have been about seven. I checked every place in my kitchen. Nothing! Finally, in desperation, I once again picked up a can of chili, which I had in my kitchen drawer for about six months. For about the fourth time, I read the label, noting the number of calories was four hundred. If the maker told the truth, it was at least five hundred, and the fat content was very high. I usually don't have this type of food this early in the morning. However, I knew now that this was to be a munch day, and I couldn't put it away. So I ate it, but not all of it. Maybe three-quarters. It was good and should have satisfied me. But it didn't.

So now what? I needed some AAA batteries and paper plates and such. I usually purchase these items at Big Lots. So I went to the computer and found out that Big Lots opens at ten on Sunday, and I waited and went, arriving as they opened the door. I got my batteries and paper plates. Did I leave then? No. I kept walking about the store, not abnormal behavior for me in this store. I found a large can of honey-baked peanuts, and I could not say no. I put it in my basket, but as I was leaving, I spotted a bag of tiny marshmallows. I had not eaten these totally unnecessary sweets in more than ten years. Munchie, munchie. I put them in my bag. As soon as I walked through my door, I opened the peanut can and started. I knew this day was going to be a disaster for me, but I seemed swept up in my voracious appetite and nibbled while I worked on the *Sunday New York Times* crossword. The results of working this puzzle would be one of my major measurements related to my assessment of the memory damage. If I found major improvements during the time that I have not smoked my shit, then I would blame my previous poor crossword solving abilities on the dope. On this particular puzzle, I am off to a good start and feel I may finish it or get very close to finishing it this week. I am not trying to tell you that this improvement is directly related to my two-week no-dope. But if I continue to do better and finish some of these difficult crosswords, it will be stronger evidence that marijuana long-term usage does not affect memory. I must not jump to hasty conclusions. Let's wait and see.

Because of all of the junk that I have eaten this day and my not going to the gym this morning, I'm thinking about a two-day fast. Thinking about it and doing it are two different things. In order to fast, I must be in a strong mindset. I have to be able to tell myself; what the f--- good are you if you can't control your appetite for two days? It is this appetite control that defines for me that I am in control, which I feel I should be. Once I make up my mind and definitely tell myself that I am going to fast, I better do it. Here it is ten in the evening, and I am still debating with myself. Should I fast, or should I have a regular diet day? My belly feels huge. I am not having good bowel movements this week. I feel stuffed and didn't get good elimination results from a Carter's pill I took earlier. I will let you know on day fifteen what I decided.

DAY 15: PSYCHOLOGICAL TEST

I had mentioned earlier that I was sleeping okay without the help of grass. Well, that is not totally true. I fall asleep with or without, but I sleep for only five hours. I would like to sleep seven hours. Using grass, I was able, after having slept my five hours, to have a few hits and sleep another hour or two. I am hoping that I, eventually, do the same without dope. I do not want to begin taking another pill.

I told you that my practice of solving crossword puzzles was an area where I felt I could make some reasonable estimates of the effects of weed. Now, I admit the aging process affects these estimates, and any statement I make regarding my addiction will be accompanied with a statement mentioning aging. Another possible evaluation technique that I thought about has entered my mind. In the year 1961, I took extensive psychological performance tests conducted by a firm called Tanner & Associates. This test was sponsored by my employer at that time, TIC (Technology Instrument Corporation). I was able to obtain a copy of the results, which I must admit were outstanding.

Dr. Tanner was a very active leader in the Mormon religion, and in 1961, I had the opportunity to visit with him and his family in his beautiful and large Pasadena home. I spoke with him, his wife, and at least two of his children, spending a half day at his home. This morning I used Google to attempt to find his firm and possibly take the tests again. Well, it turns out that Dr. Tanner passed away in 2004.

So I feel if I find the firm was taken over by someone else I, then, may be able to obtain information as to the names of the actual testing material. If I could obtain that info, find a firm in the local area that would conduct the tests, and then take them again, I would have another item to assist me in assessing the effect that forty years of dope had on my abilities while also always trying to consider the degradation caused by the aging process. I am in the process of attempting to obtain the testing data.

DAY 16: ELEMENTS OF JAZZ

It is two thirty in the morning, and I would like to sleep longer but can't seem to make it happen. So I lie in my bed, and I listen. I listen to one of my Coby MP3 players, which is loaded with my trio music. So far, not using the smoke to help me sleep another hour or two is one of the times I could break my resolution. But all of the effort I am putting into these writings has been too costly to toss out for a couple of hits.

Yesterday I completed listening to the eight lectures from the Teaching Company, titled "Elements of Jazz." It was taught by a very talented musician and a good presenter, Bill Messenger. I won't go into great detail here about my reactions to each CD in the series, only write a few words about them.

I was very happy to listen to his comments related to Frank Sinatra. They were ultra complimentary and mimicked the mental review going on in my brain as soon as he mentioned the man. I couldn't wait to communicate with Bill, and I am not sure why. Sure I wanted to tell him that he did an outstanding job, but feeling that way would not have me rush to the computer to quickly draft a letter and mail it on that same day. Part of my anxiousness was probably related to my desire to have him know some of my thoughts regarding music, in general, but also especially the thoughts that I expressed in my article called "Jazz Trios." I included a print of that article with my hastily written letter, which I had to send to the Teaching Company because I could not get Bill Messenger's address. Well, I could have if I was willing to pursue one of the "find" Web sites that charge for their services, which means that you pay for the service with your credit card. While the amount is small, which I don't mind paying, it means that another group has my credit card data, and it makes me feel insecure. So I sent my letter and "Jazz Trios" article to the Teaching Company, believing that it eventually will get to Bill.

Yesterday was also the day that I met with my Web site producer to add my art to my site. I am finding, although it may be premature, that I seem to have more energy to put into my projects. Usually I have too many going at the same time. What I'm hoping is that I, less the daily dope, will be better at finishing them and be more sensible in my expectations before I start them. So far I have been patient in the writing of this book.

DAY 17: 401K INVESTMENT

There are times when I feel like having a hit. This is one of those times. I will tell you why and give you the background. When I retired, fifteen years before writing this diary, I contributed to a 401K investment program. I was very consistent in my contributions simply because as my income increased I kept my lifestyle the same as earlier. Then in about 2002, I rolled my 401K into an IRA mutual fund. Well, I did not make much money in this plan and was very disappointed. Eventually I rolled my IRA over to CDs, which paid about 5 percent, enabling me to cover my minimum distribution and maintain my IRA amount level.

Everything was fine until the rate of interest became less than a half percent. No longer would my interest cover my minimum distribution. Because at this time the stock market seemed to have reached a bottom and was on its way up, I rolled my IRA over again. This time it was to a stock account with Scottrade as my broker. The timing of this was excellent, and I increased my account ten thousand dollars in 2009. This was more than enough to keep my account at that level while satisfying my minimum distribution requirements.

Things rolled along nicely until now; the market has become volatile and dropping, especially lately, giving me cause for concern. During the last two months, May and June, my portfolio lost about 12 percent of its value. Now I haven't truly lost because the reduction is unrealized until I sell the stocks. It is amazing how fast the stocks can retreat, compared going the other way—up. I am now at the lowest value ever for my portfolio. It seems as if many investors have gotten out of the market into what many feel is safe ground for their assets, gold. Why don't I sell, take my losses, and buy gold? Why? Because gold has reached record highs, and it would be just my luck that after I invested in it, it would turn around and come down in value, which would further reduce my portfolio value.

It was this dilemma that made me think about having a good hit. I know that any hit that I have after laying off this amount of time will result in an extra good high. It will knock me on my ass. But it wouldn't be long before that delicious type of high would disappear and my reaction to pot would be pleasant but not wonderful. If that is the case, why would I continue smoking that shit at all? Because it still makes me feel better than when I don't have some. Besides, I also consider, at this time, that this giving up my daily weed is a sacrifice. Whatever kind of crazy thinking that is, it is how I look at my addiction. Don't forget if I am successful in leaving the shit alone for, let us say, six months, then I am no longer an addict. I can take it or leave it. I know it is way too early in this endeavor to assess any major changes that I am able to measure, but as I said before, this is sort of a behavior that somehow I feel justified in receiving some kind of reward.

I have been noticing one little behavioral effect, which I believe comes from this withdrawal. It is my loss of patience for very little failures, like trying to separate two pages when reading or having difficulty taking something apart or having difficulty opening a package. I find myself giving it the "Jesus" gripe, sometimes out loud. Again, as I write about these little annoyances, I believe this knowing will help me reduce my rapid reaction of anger.

It is about two thirty in the morning. I hit the sack at nine, which you would think gives me five and a half hours of sleep. Not so, unless you can count listening to my trios as sleeping. Tonight, I reloaded one of my MP3 players—I have about six of them, one with what I call soft and slow. As I add a new trio song to my music library, I don't just rate it; I add it to a play list. Most of my additions go to my play list entitled, Best Trios. However, if I have purchased a trio's song that is slow in tempo, I add it to the play list I named Soft and Slow. Since I started doing this, I haven't played that soft and slow play list at all. The reason I created that Best Trios list is, primarily, to listen to my music at the gym.

When I'm exercising, going from one machine to another, I find it to be somewhat of a boring activity. I apply about 80 percent of my weight-handling ability to each machine. I accept that at my age I am not going to build muscle. Listen, at my age I am very happy to maintain what I have, which is part of the reason I am there. But vanity is still a strong motivator for me. I don't like looking or being fat. I believe that for many people who work out, vanity is a greater motivator, even when better health is supposedly the desire of this somewhat boring—to me anyway—activity. So the music is my boredom eraser. I probably use at least fifty calories in my one hour workout just due to my foot tapping. I would not get many foot tapping urges with my soft and slow music. So now you can understand why I made the separate play lists and why I don't want the soft and slow on my MP3 that I listen to in the gym.

So far, my son and daughter-in-law, Donna, have been supportive of my abstinence desires. They smoke but are not addicts as I am. They smoke when we get together or when they have parties with others, etc. I believe one of the key factors in considering a person to be a marijuana addict is whether he or she smokes alone. Smoking alone, certainly, or smoking before going to bed are measures of addiction.

I am heading to the kitchen now; the *Seattle Times* will be outside my door. It is Thursday, and all of the puzzles will be a little more difficult. The *USA* paper usually arrives about a half hour after the Seattle paper. This puzzle activity is important to me, not just because I enjoy the challenge and receive good feelings upon successful completions, but also because my solving abilities during abstinence may give me some sense of improvement. If it doesn't, then what? Do I consider my poor solving results due entirely to the aging process? It is way too early to know! *So hang in there, Leo; you have a long way to go.*

DAY 18: HOME-GROWN

Why did I have to pay so much for my grass when I could grow my own? I thought about growing my own shit because I had the seeds from some good stuff. I lived in the Hollywood Hills on the top floor of a house (one hundred years of age) that had a small balcony, which was somewhat hidden because of a large tree. So I bought a large tub and some good soil and planted my seeds.

I watered every day and watched my seeds sprout and start the plants' growth. Everything was going well as the plant was reaching three feet. Then it happened. This balcony is located just off my bedroom. One early evening, I thought I heard some noise out towards the balcony. I went to investigate, and there he was. A young man was climbing the tree adjacent to the balcony and had almost reached the plant.

As soon as he spotted me, he raced down the tree, and off down the street he went. Well, that did it for this plant. I couldn't let it out on the balcony so I had to bring it in and use whatever small number of leaves, not buds, that I could smoke. I never tried the balcony again.

Now I decided to make an attempt at growing some grass in my living room closet. I purchased a pulley, a set of special glow lights, two large pots, and a light-control mechanism. After setting it up, I was already getting excited about the potential of this garden, which I knew was safe from intruders. After two days, I had to tear the garden down before it really got started. What happened? I'll tell you what happened! Dumb Leo didn't think about the problems with the heat generated in that closet area, and this was August. Within a couple of days, the small growth was burned to nothing, and I had to give up again. That escapade was the last of my attempts at gardening. From then on, my dreams vanished, and I would continue to purchase my weed.

DAY 19: GOOD OLD DAYS

There was a time that many of today's prohibited drugs were available with no problem. I have taken a sample of photos of various chemical products that were touted as top-flight medicinal treatment. Now remember these products were originally introduced in the late 1890s and were sold over the counter for at least fifty years. To examine additional items not included here go to Web site www.pharmacytechs.net.

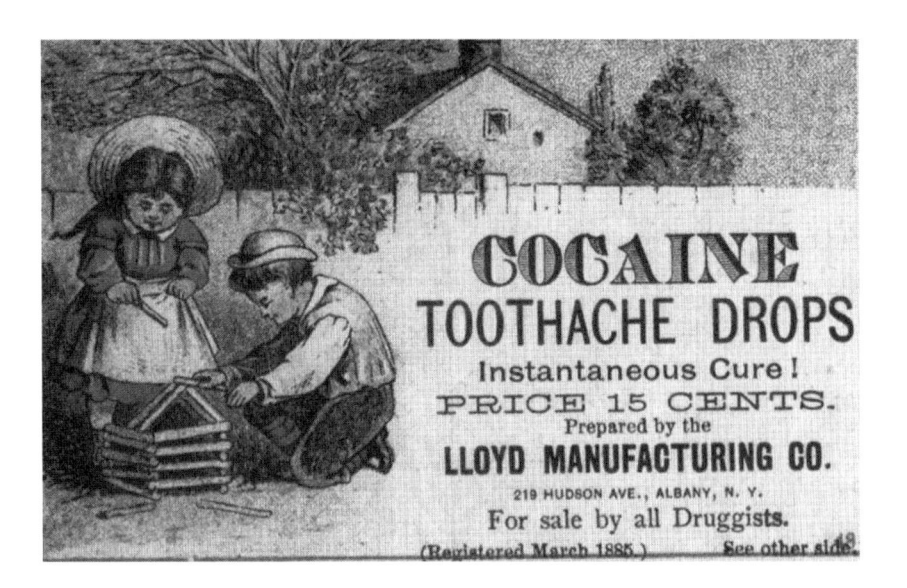

COCAINE TOOTHACHE DROPS
Instantaneous Cure!
PRICE 15 CENTS.
Prepared by the
LLOYD MANUFACTURING CO.
219 HUDSON AVE., ALBANY, N. Y.
For sale by all Druggists.
(Registered March 1885.) See other side.

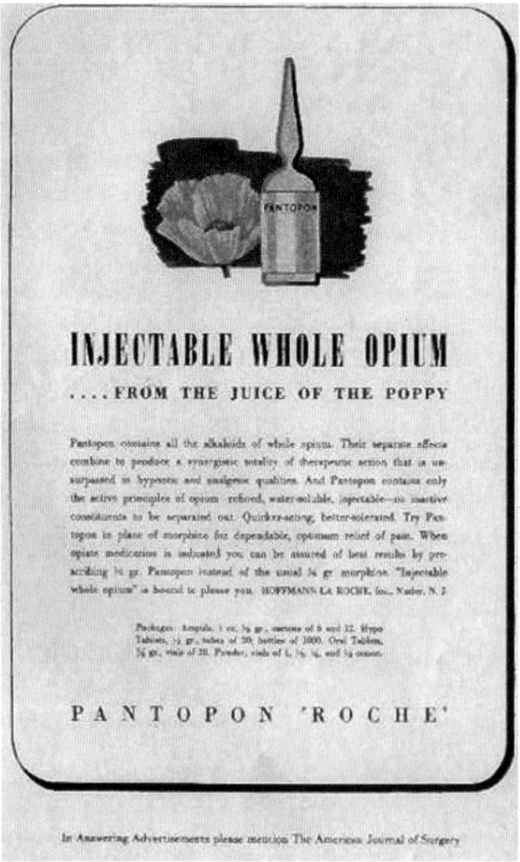
PANTOPON
INJECTABLE WHOLE OPIUM
....FROM THE JUICE OF THE POPPY
PANTOPON 'ROCHE'

FARBENFABRIKEN
vorm.
FRIEDR. BAYER & Co
ELBERFELD
Heroin
Nom déposé

COCA-COLA
SYRUP AND EXTRACT.

For Soda Water and other Carbonated Beverages.

This "INTELLECTUAL BEVERAGE" and TEMPERANCE DRINK contains the valuable TONIC and NERVE STIMULANT properties of the Coca plant and Cola (or Kola) nuts, and makes not only a delicious, exhilarating, refreshing and invigorating Beverage, (dispensed from the soda water fountain or in other carbonated beverages), but a valuable Brain Tonic, and a cure for all nervous affections — SICK HEAD-ACHE, NEURALGIA, HYSTERIA, MELANCHOLY, &c.

The peculiar flavor of COCA-COLA delights every palate; it is dispensed from the soda fountain in same manner as any of the fruit syrups.

J. S. Pemberton,
Chemist,
Sole Proprietor, Atlanta, Ga.

From fresh Coca Leaves and the Purest Wine.
Recommended for
NEURALGIA, SLEEPLESSNESS, DESPONDENCY, ETC.

For Fatigue of mind or body.
METCALF'S Coca Wine
A Pleasant Tonic and Invigorator.

THEODORE METCALF & CO.,
39 Tremont Street, BOSTON, MASS.

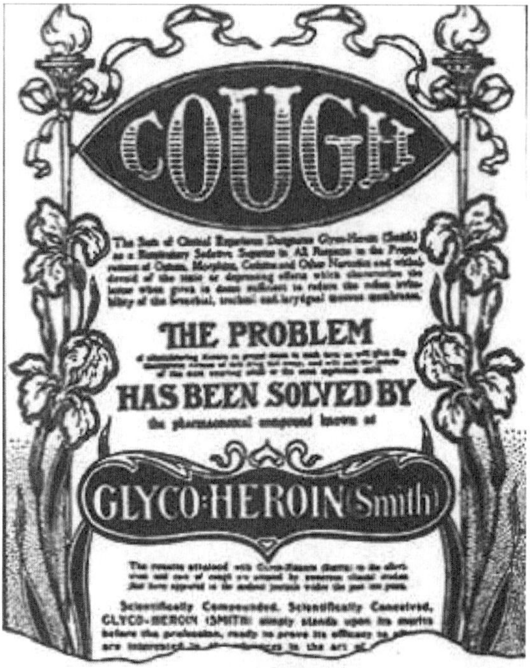
COUGH
THE PROBLEM
HAS BEEN SOLVED BY
GLYCO-HEROIN (Smith)
Scientifically Compounded, Scientifically Conceived,
GLYCO-HEROIN (SMITH) simply stands upon its merits
before the profession, ready to prove its efficacy to

For Your Health
ASTHMA CIGARETTES
SINCE 1882
For the temporary relief of
paroxysms of asthma
EFFECTIVLY TREATS:
ASTHMA, HAY FEVER, FOUL BREATH
ALL DISEASES OF THE THROAT,
HEAD COLDS, CANKER SOURS

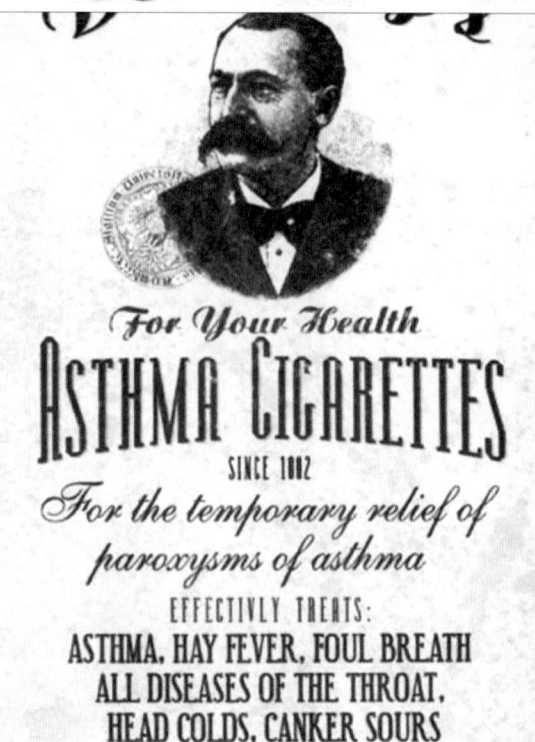

DAY 20: ECONOMICS CONSIDERED

I believe abstinence would be easier if I were busier. I spend 95 percent of my living hours at my condo. A major reason for not being out more often is my knee problem. But that's life. All of us have problems, and we have to handle them.

I am writing this diary, including my feelings during this period and also many other interests that I have now and had earlier in my life. I want to provide as much information as possible so that it can be examined, evaluated, assessed, and used by others. Who are these others? Persons who are addicts, such as I, make up one group that I believe might benefit. Persons who have a relative or friend that they believe, right or wrong, is causing himself/herself harm. Persons who are considering becoming regular users should read some of my stuff before they get in too deep. And I believe persons who are in the medical field and need more data to understand the potential harm an addict can be causing himself and whether he or she can or should stop using weed.

In addition, many states in our country have or will have laws related to medical marijuana. I would hope that, because of the possibility of legalized use of marijuana, officials federal, state, and local are interested in funding testing on the effects of the drug, which would include long-term users such as myself. I find it very difficult to accept the legal status of alcoholic beverages, also with few health tests conducted, when so much factual data regarding problems are available.

I will probably discuss my feelings about the general alcohol situation and the illegal aspect of what seems to be a much lesser problem drug, namely marijuana. Now many will say all drugs are bad. They may be correct. Let's find out more about both of these drugs so that we can make legal decisions based on laboratory and people testing.

The difficulty with any attempts to curtail the use of alcohol is the economic pressures related to all the groups that earn their living one way or another related to the use of this drug. Any major change of existing practices in our country usually affects the living means of large populations. Think of the possibility if electric cars could replace the gasoline-powered transportation vehicles of the future. For this to happen, those businesses that convert oil into gasoline, those businesses that transport gasoline, those businesses that market gasoline all will be affected in a very direct, negative way. Any major change in our culture that could put large numbers of people out of work will always meet great resistance. Consider that the legalization of marijuana could reduce our prison population by 30 percent or more. And don't forget all those police officials who are presently employed to prevent the usage of marijuana in a myriad of activities. What becomes of them? There is no doubting the economic difficulties that arise when major cultural changes occur, even though the proposed changes have been analyzed, tested, and shown to be beneficial to the general public. Change is always difficult!

Economics is very important. Consider the vulnerabilities, in addition to the cost considerations, that exist because of our need to import humongous amounts of oil. Remember the difficult and dangerous period during which there were great oil shortages. I remember it well. I had the experience of being in line for hours, and when I was about to enter the gas station for gas, the gas station ran out. It was awful. I don't want to dwell on these problems, but after that shortage period during the 1970s, I felt very strongly we should have added a special tax to every drop of oil sold. The money accumulated should have been put to use in researching alternative sources of energy. Economic conditions at that time were generally good, actually a prime time to initiate research. I don't mean to dwell on the energy policies of our country or the most likely use of electric cars. But I will dwell and persist on some kind of legalization of our drug laws.

DAY 21: PLEASURE/PAIN PRINCIPLE

Three weeks since I have smoked weed. Would I like to have a hit right now? Of course. I know that because I have a lengthy period of time since my last intake, and I know that most of the compounds that I had put in my body have now left. How do I know? Only from reading reports and stories about marijuana. I really don't feel anything different is going on with my physical being or with my brain. I do feel more energetic, at least I think I do, but it doesn't feel as if I have gone through any major change.

Because I am a loner, a non-joiner, I do not have a job, and my ailing knee prevents me from walking, I believe that I have much more time to think, I mean the kind of thinking that is free of interruption. So what do I think about? Everything except when I involve myself on a project or projects that require focused thinking. Most of the time, I am involved with activities that began from motivation that occurred during those times when I did a lot of thinking. This book or diary or whatever you want to call it is such a project. So much of my thinking these days is about this book. What shall I write about today? Since I haven't felt many physical or mental changes, which a reader of this book is primarily interested in, I would surmise, I write about those ideas and learning that I have accumulated over the years. Will they prove to be interesting to my reader? I think so, and that is part of my motivation that gives me the energy to do it.

My thoughts this day are related to my beliefs of the pleasure/pain principle. We humans have a brain, the master control of our behavior, which is free of constraint. I am somewhat controlled by the pleasure/pain principle, but I consider the human species to have a much, much lesser degree of restraint than other living things. Every living thing has three main parts. Most important is a brain, the control factor of living things. There is a group of mechanisms that we call senses, which provide input to the brain. The last component of living things is those mechanisms to which we apply the output that our control section, or brain, has processed. Those mechanisms, in humans and most animals, are the limbs.

Most modern machines function in a similar manner. Examine a few machines and their operations. Let's take a television. We control the input to the machine—we turn it on and select the channel we desire to watch. The machine has a control unit within it, usually called the computer, which receives the data, with which we, with our physical actions have provided input to the machine's brain, the computer. The machine control mechanism, the screen, provides an output based on that communication from the television's computer brain.

The basics of how living things live is comprised of those three parts—the senses, the brain, and the limbs—and how they interact. The primary difference between living things and the machine is the levels of control of the control section. Machines have a rigid response to all input from the senses, which in the case of the television set is the channel selector that we set. The living things have the ability to vary the control they apply to their limbs and their senses. There is a great difference in the level of control enabled by the brain of humans and other living animals and other living things.

DAY 22: EQUIPMENT USAGE

Tar. Tar. The word that has yet to appear in this story. What is tar? Well one thing for sure is that over the years it was something that frightened me. In Merriam-Webster's dictionary, the first listed meaning is: "a dark brown or black bituminous usu. odorous viscous liquid obtained by destructive distillation of organic material (as wood, coal, or peat)." The second meaning: "a substance in some respects resembling tar; a condensable residue present in smoke from burning tobacco that contains combustion by-products (as resins, acids, phenols, and essential oils)."

Maybe this is a good time to list the various techniques and/or equipment that I utilized to smoke grass so you can understand its connection to tar. I, like most beginners of that time (1970), rolled the weed inside a paper container, resulting in a cigarette-like container called a "joint." At first, I rolled my joints by hand, but I soon discovered I wasn't very good at this exercise. So I purchased a rolling device into which you would place the paper followed by the marijuana and, with your thumb, cause the roller to pull in the balance of the paper and wrap it about the grass. You, then, could release the joint from the rolling machine and, if needed, tighten the paper about the ends so none of the precious marijuana would fall out either end. You didn't want the grass to creep into your mouth and you didn't want the grass to fall out of the other end. At any rate, the joint was the method of choice for many years for me and those who smoked with me, although from time to time I would utilize a pipe.

The pipes that I used to smoke my stuff varied over the years. My first pipes had a metal bowl at one end and a mouthpiece at the other end. The length of this pipe was usually about three to five inches and could be purchased at what at that time was called a head shop. At these head shops, one could purchase various pipes for smoking dope. Some I will write about later. So I now had a pipe, and quite often, I had more than one in my possession. These pipes did not have any filters, and the small diameter of the passageway for the smoke, created by putting a flame by match or lighter to the bowl containing the grass, was pulled through the tiny passageway by sucking on the other end. Of course, this end that you put your lips around had a shape and material that functioned to enable you to draw the smoke comfortably into your mouth, down into your lungs, and very quickly through your bloodstream and into your brain—a passage that didn't take but seconds before you felt the sensation you were looking for.

Continuing with the description of my smoking tools, I just want to add that I often used those corn-cob pipes that could be purchased at a five-and-dime store, which were very inexpensive although they were not as hardy as the head-shop pipes. One other tool that was required if you were a pipe smoker was a stiff wire of about six inches in length that was used as a ramrod to clear any obstructions in the passageway. I have included pictures of the various devices that I used to smoke my shit.

Cool pot

One of the problems with the smoking of joints is that too much smoke is let free into the local atmosphere. If you are smoking joints at your abode, anyone entering your place will easily detect your smoking of weed because the odor of the released smoke is strong. I used to combat this problem by smoking in a closed room, which helped some. This problem also occurred when smoking with the basic pipe.

However, a short and small aluminum implement (I would not call it a pipe) was very effective in reducing the amount of smoke and accompanying odor. Because it was small, you could easily transport it in your pocket or a small purse. I have enclosed a photo of this anodized aluminum weed smoking device.

Aluminum weed smoking device

I started the writing today speaking about tar. All pot-smoking devices capture tar within them somewhere. The straightforward smoking pipe accumulates tar in the pipe pot bowl and in the passageway from the bowl to your lips. The passageway tar is difficult to remove. The stiff wire removes some of the tar so that the pipe functions but certainly not as well as when new. The wire that is used to clean the passageway collects tar that clings to the wire, giving one an example of how extensive and sticky this waste material truly is. Usually, I did not attempt to clean the wire, instead using a new wire until it became too dirty.

The examination of this wire always made me feel uneasy about my marijuana habit. If I had great difficulty in cleaning this wire, how was my body going to react to that sticky tar? Although there was tar on the bowl and the wire, I am sure that did not mean that all of the tar was captured there and not going into my body. Although I did not feel any reaction to this tar in the early years of my addiction, as the years went by, I began to cough up phlegm quite often. The stubby aluminum device also collected tar but was much easier to clean. I would remove the lip piece and the cover, which was used to load the device, leaving the central portion of the unit. Guess what I used to clean the tar in the unit? Fingernail polish remover! I would put on my vinyl gloves for this cleaning operation. I would place the fingernail polish remover in a glass and then place the tarred unit into the glass. I would allow the unit to lie in the glass for a couple of hours, shaking it every so often. But the operation of being soaked in the polish remover would not remove all of the tar. This soaking would be followed by folding a paper towel to a size that would fit into the unit now soaked with fingernail polish remover. Then I would rotate the paper towel while it was in the unit, and any tar that was not removed during the soaking process would accumulate on the towel. I would then again insert the unit into the glass with the polish remover and repeat the shaking process, remove it, again do the paper towel bit, and continue this activity until there was no more tar on the paper towels.

The units (usually I would clean more than one unit at time) were then placed into boiling water for about five minutes. I would include the flame entrance unit through the same process with the central parts of the units. After the process was complete, I would place the screens (they act as a filter, allowing the smoke, but not the grass itself, to reach your mouth) into the units and reassemble them. They were now ready to be used again.

Getting back to the original point, which I began today. Tar. Tar. I said I was concerned with the tar that was entering my body. I was concerned that someday I might find myself battling cancer in one form or another, in the throat or in the lungs. Unfortunately, there was no testing results available for this potential problem. Most of the cancer or emphysema problems that I read about involved cigarette smoking. I had a boss who was a cig smoker that lost part of his jaw to cancer. How powerful is the urge to smoke cigarettes? Do you want a prime example? I visited this man in the hospital during his recovery period, and in his facial remains was a cigarette. Awful! At that time, I was not smoking cigs, but I sure was still smoking grass. Was I concerned? Was I frightened? How could I continue to smoke? Well, I did not have any signs of a major problem. The only evidence of a problem was the phlegm that I occasionally coughed up. So I continued on my weed-smoking habit.

People who are addicts, including me, always find some means to rationalize the potential hazards of their addiction. What was my rationalization? For me, number one rationalization was that much less smoke entered my body from smoking weed than cigarettes. I was not an all-day smoker, usually only smoking in the hours after work. Even when I retired and could smoke all day if I so desired, I usually only smoked in the evening hours. My second rationalization was a belief that the body's cells die off, different cells on different cycles, and if they were not inundated with the tar, the cells could die off in their normal cycle, being replaced with new healthy cells. Sound ridiculous? To continue with my habit, which still made me feel better than not smoking this shit, I used these thoughts to continue the habit.

Why then this attempt to abstain from this daily usage? After all, I did not have any noticeable evidence of a serious problem. Primarily for two reasons. I was fearful. I wanted to give up my habit before something did show up and it was too late. Quitting now doesn't prevent a problem in the future due to my years of usage. In addition, I wasn't receiving the pleasure that I did in my earlier years. Also, I was recognizing my too-often problem, trying to remember something, and I wasn't sure if it was just a reminder that I was getting old and not the grass. But, as I say, I wasn't sure.

So now you know something about how I smoked and the devices that I used to smoke. You know more about the fear that motivated me to attempt to stop. It has only been three weeks, not enough time for any conclusions. However, for me this length of curtailment is significant.

DAY 23: HODGEPODGE

As usual, I slept well but not nearly enough. Went to bed at twelve and now it is three thirty in the morning, giving me a total of three and one half hours, of which probably one hour was listening to music. What were my thoughts that I should write about today? One was that I seem to have more energy to get things done, and the other was sort of contradictory to that, which was that I am more impatient than when I smoked grass. I also wanted to express to you, my reader, that prior to this situation I never ever kept a diary. But now beneficial to you, I do although I learned that others who are diary people usually write before retiring for the evening. I like it better to plan my day by thinking about it and writing in the morning when I rise.

I plan to fast today and tomorrow, if I can. I ate some of my favorite food that I shouldn't be eating, especially in the large quantity that I consumed. It was M&M's but not just any M&M's. It was the reddish orange package, which contains chocolate covered peanut butter. This was not the fifty-cent variety but the medium sized (so it states on the package, making me wonder that the large must be huge) one costing about three dollars. I have generally good control in avoiding sweet goodies, but those darn peanut butter with chocolate are somewhat difficult to resist. Do I have a sweet tooth? I don't know, but I am hoping that not having weed will make it easier to resist the temptations of M&M's.

Before I retired last evening, I had a peek at the stock market expectations for today, and they were not good. Actually, my expectations are also negative, not just for today but for a long time because I don't see how our economy is going to grow and provide jobs. I can't foresee anything in the near future that will alter the present dilemma. To me, the answer lies in the shifting of funds from military spending to utilizing those funds for improving our infrastructure. That is what the WPA did during our economic problems of the thirties. However, most people would agree that it was WWII that provided the impetus required to get the economy moving. I, as a child during this period, never knew there was a problem. Financially, things are okay for me at the present time and should remain so. The plan that I had in getting involved in the marketplace was to enable me to cover the costs of getting the Sielsch family together for a week or so. My guess is that it will take about ten thousand to put together an enjoyable and entertaining week for all. I guess I should mention my present market arrangement. In my IRA, all of my funds are into biotech companies, all small cap.

DAY 24: STOCK MARKET

As usual, I woke early. It is two in the morning. I fasted the last day, and my weight is down to 163 at the present moment. I have been trying for about two years to reach the 150s but have never made it, not even for a moment. If I fast today and stay away from food until tomorrow morning, I know I will have been successful, finally. Can I do it? I don't promise you or me that I will fast all day today.

My portfolio took another beating yesterday. The stock indexes were both positive, and so I thought if I had a reduction it would be minor. Boy, was I wrong. I couldn't believe it. I guess the biotechs are being hit the hardest of all sectors. Probably because almost all of my health stocks are unprofitable, meaning they haven't been making money yet. Most have some product or products in the FDA (Food and Drug Administration) pipeline, and their present stockholder support from investors like me is optimistic, to say the least. It is on my mind, and I strongly feel that my savings could be nearly wiped out. It hurts because I lived frugally in order to accumulate those funds. I don't regret those minor sacrifices that were required, but I do regret that I am now blowing a good portion of my savings. Now when I say I am a big loser, that would be if I were to sell all of the stocks that are presently in my portfolio, which I am not about to do. These losses that I write about are called unrealized losses, meaning that their present stock market values are way below the amounts that I paid for them but I haven't experienced the actual loss because I haven't sold them; it's just a loss on paper (or in my mind). The near future doesn't look rosy to me, and the situation could get much worse. What are my alternatives? I could sell everything, making my losses real, which would be one way of not going deeper in the hole. If I did that, I would lose about 15 to 20 percent of my original IRA rollover amount. If I use the portfolio's best achieved but not realized gains, my loss is about 25 percent. One thing that I have learned during this investment experience is that stocks travel twice as fast going down as when they are going up. I will tell you what my investment strategies were and still are.

I do not have a large amount of savings, which is a factor in the choices I have made. All of my stocks in my portfolio were acquired at single digit numbers. These investment choices were based on the assumption that I would have a better chance with large quantities of ten low-priced stocks than small quantities of high-priced stocks. It seems to me that if I purchased a thousand shares of a stock at a cost of four dollars the very most I could lose would be four thousand dollars. So let us say that I used my entire savings of forty thousand dollars to buy ten stocks—one thousand shares of each at four dollars per share, or a total of four thousand dollars for each stock. The most I could lose on any individual stock would be four thousand dollars. Say, instead, I used that forty thousand dollars to purchase only two higher-priced stocks—two thousand shares of each, costing ten dollars per share—my savings is invested in two stocks, each now worth twenty thousand dollars.

So I have portfolio (a) that has ten stocks, one thousand of each at four dollars, totaling forty thousand dollars. The other, portfolio (b), has two stocks, two thousand shares of each at ten dollars, also totaling forty thousand dollars. Now if a total disaster strikes one of my portfolio (a) stocks, I would lose four thousand dollars. If only a major (rather than a total) disaster occurred in portfolio (b) and one stock lost half its value, I would lose ten thousand dollars. That's an example of the risk possibilities.

Now before we look at the profit possibility of these two portfolios, I am going to take a coffee break and read the *Seattle Times*, which has arrived at my doorstep. How nice is that—I open my door, and not having to take any steps out of my condo, I reach down and pick up the paper. Coffee was brewed last evening so I pour myself a half cup (always, never a full cup because it gets cold too quickly) and place it in the microwave one minute express. It reaches a perfect drinking temp, and now to the paper.

But wait! I now have the lights on, and Tweeter is aroused and beginning his favorite morning activity of making noise. I don't remember if I told you, but most parakeets enjoy making noise and destroying things. Now I want you to know that, no matter what time of day, I try to keep the noises down. I don't like noise, and I certainly know my upstairs neighbor feels likewise. He is unbelievably quiet. When I first moved in here, during the first three weeks, I believed him to be on assignment somewhere and not home. Guess what? He was in his condo above, all of those three weeks. I was astounded! I have never lived anywhere with so little noise. I express my condo as a tomb, except for one thing, Tweeter. And when he is noisy in the early hour of three o'clock in the morning, I am disturbed. So I am going to try a new routine. I will take my coffee and my newspaper and head to my computer room, where I am now typing, which I will soon curtail so that I can enjoy my coffee and my newspaper puzzles and the news. I want to remind myself that when I come back to these writings after my coffee(s) and newspapers (the *USA* will be here shortly) I don't want to forget to tell you about the motivation needed to fast successfully. I am going back to bed. I feel exhausted. Remember I have not eaten a thing in about thirty hours.

It is now three in the afternoon. I fasted yesterday and will not have a parcel of food until tomorrow morning. In fact, I have already prepared my breakfast for tomorrow. This is, of course, my first time attempting to fast when I am not a user. It is much easier. I am so happy to find another good benefit from abstinence.

This morning—gosh, I can remember it!—I wrote of my stock portfolio problems. Wouldn't you know it? The market took a good move upward today, and every one of my stocks gained. However, the market for me works in an unfair routine. One day my portfolio goes down 6 percent. When it goes up shortly thereafter, it rises 2 percent. Over a long period of time, you can easily understand the substantial losses caused by this market volatility, and maybe this type of fluctuation is what eventually causes the finance media to condemn it as a bear market.

I have prepared two articles that I want to add to my Web site (www.imzilch.com) under the new subject, health. One article is called "Toothbrush Machines for Good Bodies." I won't go into detail on this article with a questionable or maybe even ridiculous title because I want you to visit my site. The other article has a sensible title, "Lose Weight—Gain Health." There, I have covered the most important activities to achieve and maintain good health, to wit, proper diet and regular exercise. Of course, that statement must be factored by absence of drug use. Although this druggie does not have serious health problems at this time, I believe the uncompromising application of my diet and exercise philosophies has helped me to offset the potential ill effects of my drug use. Good health to me is the absence of any major life-threatening illness and a daily presence of generally just plain feeling good, very happy and excited to greet the new day. That doesn't mean that I am free of all bodily daily aggravations that must be tended to. Shall I mention them? I might have previously in this diary, but as I said initially, there will be times I will repeat myself because of my poor memory, and that poor memory is probably the prime motivation behind my abstinence. To be honest, I miss my grass.

DAY 25: MEMORY PROBLEMS

Today is a very hot day. I didn't have the pep that I usually do working the machines in the gym. My thoughts this morning were related to my current poor memory condition. This morning, I thought back to the time that I was western regional sales manager for Perkin Elmer Corporation. One of my best customers was the Litton Corporation. We, the Electronic Products division of Perkin Elmer, had a proprietary potentiometer that Litton used on one of its gyro platforms.

There is an incident that I can remember very clearly that involved a meeting with the Litton people associated with the engineering and purchasing of the gyro platform. A vice president of our company, general offices located in Connecticut, came to attend this meeting and others at other firms. Now you must remember this is at a time in my life (my age was thirty-two) that I didn't even know what marijuana was. I told you before that I thought I had a poor memory, a thought that I think either began or was strongly reinforced by my trigonometry math courses in high school and another notice of a memory problem in my chemistry course at WPI, Wyomissing Polytechnic Institute. So I was well aware of my memory situation, and to top it off, the worst was remembering names, which is still my greatest problem. So while driving to pick up the VP, I studied the names of some of the people from Litton who would attend this meeting. I didn't use a tactic to help me in this particular meeting, which I usually would, because of the presence of the VP. I would print part of the names of the people I was to meet with on my wrist, small and hopefully unnoticeable. The point of my telling you this story is to make you and me understand that I really always had some memory problems. So I tell you again that a major motivation in this abstinence was the fear of Alzheimer's and the hope that not smoking my shit would help in preventing my drifting into an Alzheimer's illness big time. That's it for today on that subject.

DAY 26: PHILOSOPHY

Have I given you the feeling that I don't have a strong urge to have a hit? To cheat and not write about it? A long time ago, I learned that one of the most terrible things to do is to lie to yourself. Of course, I have an urge. But the function of these writings is to strengthen my resolution. There is an awful lot going on in the marijuana world. There are medical marijuana sellers in many of the states operating legally by state law but not by federal law. Don't you think a major factor in the legalization must concern limitations, primarily regarding children, just like alcohol?

If I remember correctly, the English, when they were very powerful in India, felt that the weed would affect the workers in what they considered a negative way. They wouldn't produce. So they worked hard to curtail its use in India. I am here to input my story after forty years. Look at my record. Abstinence is a word that to me does not mean forever. The forever bit comes into play when the book is finished. What's the old saying, "no harm, no foul"? At this point, I don't have any notion as to how this will all play out. Right now as I write, I can only know that I cannot make any conclusions after twenty-six days. I believe that after sixty days I will know where I am, related to my general health and welfare.

In the meantime, I am going to write of my philosophies and experiences. After all, I am an old man, and I hope a wise old guy. You will be the one to make any judgment as to the value of the info I am revealing to you.

I will be telling you of my philosophy of life. We all have our philosophies, which guide our behavior. I have more time to think about my philosophy of life and to write a book such as this. And I have spent many years as a loner, not writing but reading. Reading all non-fiction. Learning, I hope.

DAY 27: TOOTHBRUSH MACHINES

I probably mentioned it before so I will be brief. I get those days when my appetite drives me to eat everything that's available. It doesn't take grass to make me vulnerable to a munchie day.

Yesterday I visited with the people who have mastered my Web site. I added a new item, health. Two articles will be on my site by Monday; today is Saturday. The first article related to exercise is titled "Toothbrush Machines." (Yes, I shortened it from what I told you a few days ago.) I know it is a strange title, but the article itself is not strange, just different. In it, I relate the regularity that people apply to the care of their teeth to the need to apply such a regimen toward their body. I won't go into detail here; please visit my site (www.imzilch.com).

The other article is really pointed toward those of us who don't eat enough vegetables. I am one of those, and based on all of the evidence accumulated over many years and numerous tests indicating the health benefits of having veggies in one's diet, I had to change my ways. I did! This article is titled "Eat Less—Gain Health." It explains the method that I used to include in one week as many veggies that I used to eat in two months. If you don't have very many vegetables in your diet, or you just don't like them, please visit and read this article. I do not anticipate any additional items to my site, prior to the completion and publication of this diary, except for humorous videos.

My oldest son and I are going to attempt to create a video using Walter, Jim Denham's dummy doll that my son gave me for my birthday. We are attempting to reverse the roles, making Walter the ventriloquist and me the dummy. I am looking, acting, and speaking more like Walter every year so I shouldn't have any difficulty playing the part. The first problem we encountered was obtaining a doll resembling any male who could be the ventriloquist that was small enough to sit on Walter's lap. Remember that Walter is now the ventriloquist, standing and holding the dummy, that's me, in his arms. The Walter dummy, the ventriloquist in this parody, is about sixteen inches tall, and we think we have found two possible dummies. One is eight inches tall, and the other is six inches tall. After my son and I examine the Web site offering these dolls and discuss the pluses and negatives, and if the positives win, we will purchase the dolls, which are not expensive anyway. I will keep you informed on our progress. We both feel that if we can pull this off and get the video onto YouTube we have a good chance of a great increase in visitors to our Web sites.

And that brings up another issue. Should I include sketches, drawings, and photos in this diary? Normally diaries do not. I am not going to make that decision today, even though I do feel that pics and such make a book more interesting, breaking the monotony of text. The decision is in limbo for now.

Yesterday, being a Friday, was Sudoku tough-day-of-the-week, with two five-star puzzles. Well the four weeks sans weed certainly did not make it easier to solve them. I struggled and did not finish either of the two. Wouldn't it be an interesting observation to find that I was a better solver of Sudoku when loaded than without weed? We have lots more puzzles to solve before we can conclude anything.

How is my abstinence holding up? Do I ever feel like giving up this diary and just relaxing? After all, I am proving that I can quit, even if it's just for a month. If I did get back into using, would all of the time and effort I put into this diary be a waste? No, and besides, I will not stop now. If I stop, I will have demonstrated, at least for this addict, that abstinence is difficult. So let's continue.

DAY 28: LOVE AND LIFE

A month has now gone by, and I am still hanging in there. A month. I would like to finish this diary on a positive note another month from now. I believe that if I can achieve an abstinence period of two months I will no longer consider myself an addict. What will I do after I reach that stage? Will I start all over? Or is it true that once an addict, always an addict? I quit cigarettes when I was about fifty. Up until that time, I would have to be considered an addict. Was I suffering from my cigarette addiction? No. I was married at the time to a woman fifteen years younger than I. She also was an addict; we quit together. We both knew that this nicotine habit was not good for us. Her name is Barbara. I loved her very, very much. It was the fifteen years, starting at age twenty for her and age thirty-seven for me, of having her in my life that was and still is the major basis for my satisfaction with my life on this planet Earth. I always thought that we would be together forever. But now, when I review my behavior during our time together, I am fortunate that she stayed with me as long as she did. When we parted, I cried. Even today, twenty-six years since our parting, I still tear, at times, when thinking of her. Even though we parted and she had a new person in her life, I always thought we would be friends forever as long as we both were alive. She has been with that person, Doug, ever since we parted. They married, but I don't remember exactly when that was. I was not a good husband; in fact, I was a controlling asshole who was lucky to have her remain with me as long as she did. I often wonder if she were to write about me what those writings would reveal.

We only contact each other on our birthdays, usually by telephone. We did remain in touch for at least ten years after we parted. Then the telephone calls from Barbara became emails. I believe she was experiencing panic attacks and began taking Prozac or a similar medication and that changed our relationship. It surely wasn't my choice. I am almost positive that a horrible incident that occurred during our relationship arose in her mind a number of years afterward and caused her great pain and suffering. The incident I speak of was rape, but it was even worse than rape because of the circumstances involved. I am not going to write a great amount about this terrible happening except to say it involved the very good possibility that her life would be taken from her. She was raped by two young men, both black. The color of your skin doesn't affect the terror involved.

In order for you to understand what she went through, I am forced to tell you some of the details. I believe it was either a Friday or Saturday evening, and Barbara went out to be with the girls. It was not an uncommon outing, nor was her going out without me uncommon. I was not much for drinking or being out where people drank alcohol. The older I got, the less I liked it. Don't get me wrong. As a kid in my teens and early twenties, I did it, but I never drank very much and was particularly disgusted with many party drinkers and never enjoyed their company. What they called fun, I didn't. You must understand I grew up and spent from age seven to age seventeen living in a bar. And it was a low-class bar, not a cocktail lounge.

Even now, about thirty years after the rape, I have difficulty writing about it.

I can imagine why she would want the memory of it out of her life forever. This lady, Barbara, was the most giving and caring and unselfish person that I have ever met. To have this happen to such a wonderful human being is so, so unfair. I don't feel up to continuing with this chapter of our lives together. I will tackle it again later. I feel better now. I will write about Barbara and that terrible incident another time.

I went back to bed, thinking of people in my life that were gentle, caring, and never displayed, at least to me, much that could be called "sin." Larry Bunker was such a person. Larry was the husband of Brandyn. I was more of a friend to Brandyn, actress, singer, and cancer survivor with a one woman show, *Sister Girl*, than I was to Larry. During the years from 1970 till 2004, I visited and spent more time in the Bunkers' home than any other. When they went on a vacation to Europe, I lived in their house for weeks. It was beautiful. I tell you of Larry Bunker for a number of reasons. Fate determined that I would come to be friends with this musical talent who played various instruments professionally, who it was said had the best ear in the studio orchestras for many years, and who was an early West Coast jazz icon. It was the year 1950, and I was attending school at Wyomissing Polytechnic Institute. I was supplementing my income by dealing cards for seven-card poker at a local card joint in my home town of Reading, Pennsylvania. I usually worked on Friday evening or Saturday evening. On Saturday evening, the card joint's proprietor had some kind of arrangement with the city officials. He would always shut down the game at about three o'clock Sunday morning, sometimes to the dismay of the game's losers who were very disappointed that they didn't have the opportunity to get even. Nonetheless, Johnny Cutler, I believe, was the man who ran the game, and my thinking is that the city official(s) wanted the place shut down before the church-going people hit the streets in the early morning on Sunday.

It was a true joint with a constant cloud of second-hand smoke. Everybody smoked in a card game like this, one cig after another, playing seven cards down the river poker, a game, which usually had ten players and two dealers on a rotating half-hour routine. The dealer monitored the game, removing 5 per cent from each pot, somehow unobtrusively. Then as a dealer, I was paid a percentage of those moneys that I collected during my time as a dealer that evening and morning.

Sometimes after the closing at three in the morning, some of the gambling participants and I went a half block or so to an after-hours club. There generally weren't many winners in this poker game. Figure it out. If every pot has 5 percent removed from the game, eventually it would cause the overall betting moneys to decline considerably, resulting in a situation where there could be no winners. What saved that from happening was a constant flow of new income; additional players entered the game as the evening wore on.

On this one particular Sunday morning, I went to the club, which had a jukebox that offered the kind of music that was rather uncommon in this laid-back town of a population of a hundred thousand. Country and top pop were to be found in most jukeboxes of local bars and restaurants. I was a music lover, but my speed was radio late at night where I could get stations from Philadelphia and somewhere down south; I don't remember the city. The music I desired to listen to was big band and jazz. So here I am in this after-hours club, noisy as hell since most people were drinking and in partying moods. I remember that I was sitting at the bar, taking in the scene, watching the goings on, but not really participating. A number came up on the jukebox, which featured a trumpet player whose technique was new to me. I was the fan of some of the big band trumpeters like Harry James and others whose names I have forgotten. (Just as a quick aside, I saw Harry James at the Palladium in Hollywood about two months before he passed.) Impressed by this new take on the number at the club, I listened rather intently to this trumpeter and enjoyed his sound and method. Never heard him again for years. I didn't go to this after-hours club often. For one thing, I was about seventeen and shouldn't have been allowed to be there, and there were some shady characters amongst the patrons. So it wasn't till many years later, probably ten, at which time I was now living in California, that I learned that the trumpet player was Chet Baker. He played in a quartet, which at that time was a leader in what was called "cool West Coast jazz," which included groups like Dave Brubeck's quartet. I did not like the East Coast small group music led by the well-known saxophonist, Charlie Parker. These groups, mostly centered in New York City, played bop. I abhorred it! I couldn't believe it was popular. I won't go into why I disliked it at this time because I want to get back to the fateful story about Larry Bunker.

Besides Chet Baker on the trumpet, this recording at the after-hours bar also had Gerry Mulligan, a well-known sax player on the baritone sax. I don't remember the bass player. Guess who was the drummer! You're correct. It was Larry Bunker. What a small world. And over the years, I would attend various jazz cafes in the southern

California area where Larry was performing. However, Bunker had somewhat left the small group jazz scene to become a studio musician, primarily working on sound tracks for films as a timpanist, playing a great variety of all of the instruments in that category. Of course, he played for the best of Hollywood's musical film composers and conductors. The point of this story, again, is that you never know; life can be strange.

As I said earlier, Larry was a gentle sinless person, and he was at one time an alcoholic. Wanting to limit the temptation to drink was part of his leaving the jazz scene and entering the less-travel-no-drinking music life of film production. However, there were times, in the evening while visiting with Brandyn, that I found Larry partaking of some wine. This was in his later years when he was in his sixties or seventies but still working. His whole demeanor was quite different on these evenings when he had a little too much. He was not drunk, just different. His speech was somewhat slurred, and I felt uncomfortable being around him. There were signs of bitterness that I never had ever noticed before. These were sometimes directed toward his wife, Brandyn. It was somewhat pronounced to me because in all the years of being around him before, I never ever had witnessed such behavior. It didn't happen often, but my feelings about alcohol were very negative.

DAY 29: MODERATION

I went to the gym yesterday, a Sunday, and I forgot my gym gloves, my music headphones, and most important, my wallet. I haven't done such a thing for at least two years. So, can I relate this forgetting in some manner to my "no smoke"? I don't think so. It happened because I was tired. I didn't sleep well Saturday evening and Sunday morning. No reference, as far as I am concerned, to my abstinence.

However, I had great difficulty with the Sudoku five-stars this weekend, but lo and behold, I am doing extremely well on the *New York Times* crossword puzzle. All in all, I believe it is way too early to make any inferences in such a short number of days. Let's see what happenings occur as we get further down the road. I had a very brief dream that I had a hit while riding on a bus or somewhere and others taunted me. I felt terrible that I had given in to have a hit. Even a few puffs would spoil my abstinence. I was so happy when I realized it hadn't happened!

My daughter lost one of her best girl friends. On Saturday July 10, 2010, her friend JD committed suicide. They had been friends for over twenty-five years. I met her about twenty-five years ago. She was an attractive, delightful lady. She was fifty-two at the time of her death. My daughter told me that JD and her husband of twenty years had not been getting along for many years. My daughter doesn't know all of the details. She is traveling to New Mexico, JD's home, to assist in final preparations because JD did not have active communication with her family. My daughter will visit with us here in Lynnwood, probably by next Sunday. Even though I knew JD mainly from the stories that my daughter told me over the years, I still was shaken that such a young person, only fifty-four, would take her life.

So after twenty-nine days, the greatest challenge to my resolve seems to occur when I have sleep problems. I am not sure why it is that when I can't seem to fall asleep I have the thought that if I have a hit I will immediately fall asleep. I must be more patient. Imagine if I had pains that would be gone if I had some weed. Why, I would definitely find it much more difficult to stop using. But I don't have any sensations that bother me. All in all, the main notion I have is related to missing out on the pleasant feelings from smoking the shit. Although I still enjoy my music, I do notice a lessening of the sensations I felt when high. At least that is what I can remember.

When my son and daughter-in-law were here at my place for our regular pizza and spinach salad dinner, my son had a hit or two. It did not faze me in any way. Both of them are smoking cigs after many years of not doing so. I asked my son and his wife what quantities they smoke. My son smokes very few cigs, maybe three or four a day while Donna smokes a quarter of a pack a day. They never smoke in the house, always in their garage. I never saw either of them smoke. Would I like to smoke? Yes, I would enjoy a Sherman or two, but I am so afraid that even a puff would either start me at it again or cause my body to react in some horrible way. I cannot have even a puff.

I remember that period in my life during which I had gone sixteen years without a cig. I was so sure of myself that I accepted the offer of a female friend to join her in a smoke or two. That was the beginning of the end of my prolonged absence from nicotine. I soon got started again. How stupid of me.

DAY 30: POT LOOK-ALIKES

I want, again, to tell you that I may repeat some of the stories that I tell you in this diary. My memory, in my estimation, is poor. How poor in comparison to the average person my age, I cannot say. So I will go on. Today's thoughts are about the marijuana look-alikes. This came up because of a number of articles in the newspaper and possibly on the Web. A new substitute is a synthetic variety, of which I will tell you more later today after I Google for more info.

But first, I will tell you of my experience with another grass that is not cannabis. I don't remember its name, but I had read about it, as usual, in the newspaper. Apparently, some states, Florida being one, were considering making it illegal. At the time of my involvement with this dope, it was legal. That legality was the prime reason for me to try it. Wouldn't it be nice not to have to be so secretive? Again, I don't know its name, but I will find the name and facts about the synthetic. … I found it easily with the help of Google, but it is two in the morning, and I just don't have the wherewithal to get into that story and the stories that I found about "marijuana withdrawal." If you Google that term, you will receive 12,700,000 results. Wow, and I thought I was a pioneer of sorts. Well, I don't think I will find that many withdrawals of forty-plus-year addicts presenting their story over a long abstinence period.

DAY 31: WITHDRAW AND PREPARATION

I found this site titled "marijuana withdrawal." It opens with the definition of withdrawal: "the collective symptoms that occur when a drug is abruptly withdrawn and known as withdrawal syndrome and are often the only evidence of physical dependence."

It goes on to say, "The symptoms of marijuana withdrawal include but are not limited to: Irritability, anxiety, physical tension, decreases in appetite and mood, stomach pain, restlessness, anorexia, increased aggression, strange dreams."

Not listed in this group is the desire to partake of some. Maybe it is a mistake for me to have grass readily available. And in the form ready to insert into my aluminum pipes (not really pipes but look at the pictures that I have included). I probably neglected to mention the methods I use to prepare my marijuana buds for smoking.

About twenty years ago, I purchased a very expensive kitchen tool, a whole food machine, named "vita-mix total nutrition center." It is a food grinder of great strength (stainless steel blades). It comes with a recipe directory containing directions for a multitude of food combinations, all to be prepared by placing the foods into the container with the blades. The controls offer variable speeds of operation. For years and years, I used this device to prepare what I believed was a very nutritious juice. My ingredients were carrots, spinach, and pineapple. This machine, under my control, ground these items to a drinkable form, not strained but providing the full benefits of their fibers in addition to the juices. As I said earlier, there are many nutritious combinations easily prepared with this device. My first utilization of the machine was to prepare some "loaded" chocolate chip cookies. Prior to having this device in my kitchen, I would prepare the grass by hand for its eventual mixing with the chocolate chip dough. Unfortunately, the grass was not in a powder form and was easily noticed both by looking and/or eating the marijuana laced cookie after it was baked. Well, when the grass was placed in the mixer machine, it could be ground to a powder, which when mixed with the dough was unnoticeable. Soon thereafter, I began using this machine to prepare my marijuana for smoking. I removed all of the strong stems from the buds and just placed the buds in the machine. I then controlled the speed to arrive at the composition of the grass I desired.

Despite my experiment in abstinence, I have in my possession some weed still in the "bud" state, having done nothing with it, still the same as when I purchased it. I feel strongly that if I didn't have these writings, which hopefully will end up as a well-sold book, I would lose my resolve and have some. This book is a powerful motivator, especially since I now have so much work invested in it. This is only day thirty-one. Will I hold out until day sixty? What will I have to write about on all of those days? Nobody, but nobody knows that I am working on this diary book. No one!

DAY 32: JOY CHANGES

I have been doing very well on the daily Jumble puzzle contained in the *Seattle Times*. I like the feelings when I am able to pull the correct word from the mixed up letters given. Although I cannot reach any major conclusions about marijuana's effect on my brain, I will monitor as best as I can. I feel okay about my daily crossword-solving abilities, but again, I can't say that I am making some sort of breakthrough in them. *Have patience, Leo.*

I sometimes think about the exposure of my addiction. People that I have worked with for years will now know. People that I exercise with every day will now know. My family already knows so that is no problem, and that is what really counts.

I spent some time on the Web yesterday, trying to get some solid information about the creation of stem cells that could be needled into my knee. Although the procedure is not approved in this country, it is being performed in Germany and Mexico. However, when I search and search for those people who have had this operation and will talk about it, I find none. If I could find two or three people who have had stem cells inserted into their knees and I felt that their disclosures were favorable and honest, I would definitely pursue that operation myself. So for now, all I can do is try to keep up-to-date on the progress of this approach to knee problems. I received in the mail today my copy of the *Smithsonian*. I began paging through it, and in the early pages are the letters to the editor. There was a letter titled "Today's Prohibition." I am going to print it here in its entirety, also giving you its author.

> Daniel Okrent's account of alcohol prohibition (the book *The Man Who Turned Off the Taps*) is very instructive and relevant to our current marijuana prohibition and the failed war on drugs. The nation realized the idiocy of alcohol prohibition after 13 years and repealed the constitutional amendment, but the idiocy of the present prohibition of marijuana has persisted for decades. This policy has resulted in marijuana arrests totaling at least half of all drug arrests and thousands of people being incarcerated for "nonviolent" drug crimes. Hundreds of people have been killed in Mexican cartel's drug-related violence. The United States must come to its senses: legalize, tax, and regulate marijuana. The revenue could be used to treat people who have serious substance abuse problems with drugs, alcohol, and tobacco.
>
> Edwin L. Stickney, MD
> Billings, Montana

I am certain that I have read many other letters and magazine articles advocating the legalization of marijuana, especially in the last few years. I myself have written, but not submitted, similar letters. Will my diary of my experiences of over forty years of using marijuana and the day-to-day feelings and various symptoms during my withdrawal period be useful? I sincerely hope so. I hope that this exposure of the history of my use of this prohibitive drug will cause thinking among my readers—those that are using, those that are thinking about using, and those in the medical field who are trying to assess the effects of long-term usage.

When in this withdrawal process should I wrap up this diary and expose myself to all as a longtime user? When will I be satisfied that all symptoms, both good and bad, arriving from this non-using period have occurred and been exposed? Today, the thirty-second day, is too soon. I can say at this point in the withdrawal that those articles and stories claiming that marijuana withdrawal does not produce bodily irritations are correct. The thing that I notice the most is the lasting desire, once again, to have a smoke and get that good feeling that is still strong in my daily thoughts. Will that eventually fade away? I don't think so. I think it will be very similar to the feelings that I have had and still have since I withdrew from cigarette smoking over four years ago. I'll always want some.

Discontinuing actions that gave me good feelings, that didn't result in negative day-to-day reactions, will always be somewhat regretted. Usage of drugs that makes one feel good without any associated ill feelings is difficult to stop. It takes a very strong belief in the potential long-term harm that could be caused in order to withdraw. Unfortunately, my own experiences as outlined in this book will not provide the kind of knowledge that would make one want to discontinue its use. My experiences may even encourage non-users to begin using.

To me there are many inputs to our bodies that make us feel good that take a great deal of time (years) to affect our bodies in a negative way. For me, it was such items as ice cream and many sweet foods. Discontinuing these items from my daily eating habits was just as difficult as discontinuing marijuana. It was the abundance of knowledge from the medical testing of various foods that was the primary reason for me to stop eating them. I never felt ill from their use although the effect on my body's anatomy—getting fat—concerned me. Was it vanity that was the motivation, or was it the evidence from medical tests? I believe it was a combination of both. The abstinence of cigarettes was motivated, on one hand, by actual evidence (coughing up phlegm) and, on the other, by horrors I saw others experience from cigarette smoking (my ex-mother-in-law died of lung cancer); both provided strong motivation to stop. The withdrawal of cigarettes did not cause me any pain or major discomfort. It was legal to smoke so that was not a factor in my quitting. The cigarette habit was no more costly than the marijuana habit, so that was not a strong pusher for quitting. So why did I quit smoking? Simply because the evidence of potential painful illnesses and maybe even death made me stop what was a pleasurable habit.

I don't have that strength of motivation to quit my marijuana habit. I have to go back to my belief in the pleasure/pain control mechanisms. I am very fearful of Alzheimer's disease. Every day I experience some memory problems. Are they the natural result of the aging process? Are they caused by my grass habit? I do not know. That is something I hope to learn more about as a result of a long-term abstinence. The problem is that a measurement of one's memory abilities is not simple, although I am sure that there are scientifically designed memory tests available. Usually they measure short-term memory abilities. As I have stated previously, I believe my long-term crossword solving experiences will give me some evidence.

I believe that nothing is forever except death! What does that mean, and how do I apply that belief in my life? It means that all of life's experiences, good and bad, do not last forever. Whether they be the most joyful experiences or the most miserable, they will end. I had a number of years of the most pleasurable, the most joyful times, those greatest of extreme good feelings, those seconds of sexual release. They came after the most miserable period of many years in which I suffered from sexual dysfunction.

Also, as you recall, I injured myself as a young boy of fifteen years of age. I had been a very active young boy who loved all sports activities. I had participated in baseball, football, tennis, ice skating, bowling, hiking, water skiing, basketball, etc. After that accident, I had to discontinue all of those pleasant and joyful activities forever. Of course, I tried to participate but found that I only aggravated my injury and thus would be somewhat incapacitated for some time afterward. Fortunately, I was able to continue bowling and even though I could not make a proper golf swing, I was able to play golf for many years. At the present time in my life I no longer can walk more than a few blocks. After my childhood knee injury, I could no longer run, but I could walk. Walking became my most pleasurable hobby. I walked and walked over many years, on and off the golf course. I found other pleasures in life because I accepted that which I could not change.

When faced with the ending of a joyful habit or hobby I used the following:

DON'T BE SAD. BE GLAD FOR WHAT YOU HAD!

Probably the greatest hurt of my life was the loss of my wife after the most wonderful fifteen years of laughter and joy in my life. Believe it or not, I am at peace within myself because I have had that wonderful experience with a wonderful woman. I had more joy and laughter during those years than in all the other years of my life. That doesn't mean I didn't have other good relationships and pleasurable years. I don't know how "Superman" Christopher Reeve or super-brain Stephen Hawking, both inflicted with terrible bodily malfunction situations, managed, I believe, to find joy in their lives.

DON'T BE SAD. BE GLAD FOR WHAT YOU HAD!

DAY 33: SEPTUAGENARIAN SEX

Woke up early again. It is now two in the morning. I have been watching the British Open for the last hour, but I am going to return to bed soon. Hurting back this morning, most probably overdid my exercise on one of my favorite machines yesterday. When things are going well with my exercise, I sometimes get the feeling of invincibility and then overdo it. I'm thinking of applying heat when I return to bed. Remember this is Friday, tough Sudoku day, which I always look forward to.

DON'T BE SAD. BE GLAD FOR WHAT YOU HAD!

I already used these words as they related to my wonderful fifteen years with Barbara. I previously mentioned my erectile dysfunction problems, which became noticeable at age fifty. When I started having difficulty maintaining an erection, I was confused and frightened. I had no problems with my libido for I was always hot to trot. And Barbara had put the rape behind her, or so I thought at that time. She was as warm as ever. But as my erections seemed more difficult to achieve and definitely almost impossible to maintain, I began to think. Maybe after so many years with B., I could be getting sexually bored and need new stimulation. I felt as much love and joy with my darling wife, but I still had the erection problems when I got involved with a young lady for a late evening rendezvous. Another failure. The only thing I learned was that even though my libido was aroused by this new adventure, my erection problems continued. How sad. I got mixed up in some sex play that could have put the final touch on my marriage. As I have written earlier, the bedroom problems were probably the final force that caused my mate to stray and fulfill her needs. At age fifty-two, was ED going to end my sexual activities for the rest of my life?

I had learned of the injection of special compounds into my penis and had finally experienced great sex with a very hard hard-on. After a number of pleasurable years together with the young woman who was so helpful in my using the injection method and having good sex, I realized that we had no real long-range togetherness in our future. I was sixty-eight; she was thirty-four.

It was a very good time. It was a time when I needed someone to love. It was a time that inspired me to write a poem. Now, I am not a poet, and in fact, I can't even remember the exact poem without looking at the words. It was a tough task. But I feel good about it, so good that I am going to give you the opportunity to assess my attempt at love poetry. So I give you:

ROMANTIC NUANCES

ROMANCE BEGINS

In this millennium of two thousand and one,
A pleasurable relationship has begun.
Here's looking to a rewarding year of fun,
With pleasant memories when it's done.

A young woman and a senior man in a fling,
Where affection and caring are king,
With delight and mirth the two will swing,
Both savoring the bliss of doing their thing.

Of course, both are taking a chance,
For this liaison is subject to circumstance.
But hopefully their closeness will advance
And result in a mutually memorable romance.

So starting from this new millennium date,
Their behavior will determine their fate.
With passion and tenderness they dedicate
To jointly achieve a union they will celebrate.

ROMANCE STUMBLES

A pleasurable relationship was our desire.
To enjoy our togetherness we did aspire.
Wonderful memories we did acquire,
But our time of delight soon came to expire.

A young woman and a senior man confident
That all obstacles would be no detriment,
For in this partnership caring was president,
But our time of delight soon came to be spent.

A fulfillment of needs was our primary concern.
To share and assist would provide a gratifying return,
To physically and intellectually improve and learn,
But our time of delight soon came to adjourn.

A sense of security on which one could depend,
Was the requirement they were unable to transcend.
Thus as pledges reneged and broken promises portend
Soon brought our time of delight to a near end.

ROMANCE RECOVERS

At the December of this millennium year,
This pleasant relationship seems especially dear.
Those wonderful experiences we now revere.
Where, where do we go from here?

The young woman and the senior man are aflame,
As passions of affection and caring soon came
And new pledges made to continue the same.
What now, we ask, becomes of this game?

Those marvelous joys and pleasure we have found.
Countless moments of intimate closeness abound.
Unexpected compatibilities continue to astound.
What could ever cause this ship of love to go aground?

So we start the new year with the best of intent,
To continue the mating that is so magnificent.
As we go forward, our fate seems to be imminent.
It is time to make our togetherness more permanent.

ROMANCE FADES

The young woman and the senior man were with hope replete,
Began the new year with desires that were so sweet,
A sense of togetherness from which there was no retreat.
Whatever could cause this union a sorrowful defeat?

Both partners contributing their very, very best
To graciously and gladly fulfill the other's request,
Spiritually, physically, and intellectually we did invest.
Whatever could cause this union to fail in its quest?

Unshakable trust and sincere respect will never fade.
The young woman and senior man were never afraid.
Nothing, but nothing, could rain on their parade.
Whatever could cause this union to not make the grade?

Romantic relationships are difficult, and that's a fact.
Behavioral confrontations require tremendous tact.
Unfortunate differences made an unresolvable impact.
Whatever could cause this union to end did so in the first act.

ROMANCE ENDS

Three years of pleasant togetherness we did attain.
But now the tenderness and warmth are on the wane.
The presence of doubt ignites the fires of pain.
Will we ever awaken our precious love again?

How do we accept the decay of a love so grand?
What can we do to lessen the hurt and understand?
Relationships are not forever and eventually demand
The once unfathomable necessity to soon disband.

Can the senior man and the young woman recognize
The opportunity to act in a manner so wise,
To reflect and transcend beyond love's demise,
And make eternal friendship the ultimate prize?

Unfortunately, there is no relationship school.
We have to accept that there is no special rule.
Thus the young woman must maintain her cool,
And the senior man must not behave like a fool.

    I had resided at the same house in Whitley Terrace for over thirty years. For some of those years I had a young lady who cleaned for me, both before my breakup and afterward. She eventually found the love of her life and moved to Idaho with him. I searched for a replacement and found some ladies that were interested in cleaning my abode for me. I asked that they come every two weeks and normally would complete the day's cleaning in about four hours. Unfortunately, none of the interested cleaning ladies worked out. So I decided I would take care of cleaning my apartment myself. I did not do a very good job, but I lived with it. After about a year of trying to keep my abode in order and clean, I received a phone call from my friend Brandyn, asking if I would be interested in having Elia clean for me. Apparently, Elia had had some type of operation that would make it very difficult to do all of the work that Brandyn had in her large house. Elia did not speak any English, which worried me some, but after the good recommendations from Brandyn, I decided to have her clean for me. Friday was the day for cleaning in the morning from eight to noon every two weeks.

Elia had two children, both female, ages six and eight, when she first started cleaning for me. When the children were off from school on a Friday, Elia would bring them along, and they always behaved themselves well, doing homework or reading while their mother worked. Although the language situation caused some minor problems, all in all, my apartment looked great. I was dating during the years that Elia cleaned, and many times my date would stay over and be there when Elia was working. No problem for her or for me. Elia was always punctual, possibly because she lived about two blocks away and could walk to my place.

Elia was approximately thirty-eight years old when she started, and I was retired and sixty-five years of age. Elia always dressed ultra conservative, usually in jeans and long-sleeve tops. I never really looked at her except as a good cleaning lady and good mother. Then, after she had been with me for about seven years, it happened. Somehow, we embraced. It was a warm and sensitive hug that each of us knew was going further. And it did. We began a pre-cleaning activity consisting of the best sex of my life. I believe there were a number of reasons that this relationship fulfilled my dreams for a great sexual togetherness. Most of my adult life, I found myself more apt to have my libido become warm in the early morning. I believe that a male's testosterone is at its peak in the morning. In addition, we only had sex on Friday mornings when Elia came to clean, which gave us two weeks to grow our enthusiasm gradually for what was to come.

I had often heard the expression that "you don't have to know the language," and I can now tell you, from experience, that is true. Somehow the moves and changes occurring during our intercourse were negotiated without one word, especially after we had been together a few times. It also was fun for me because I could use all of the "dirty talk" freely without any repercussions since she didn't understand a word I said.

Now I told you earlier about my injection technique. So on every other Friday, I would be all prepared to inject myself as soon as I let her in. In addition to the injection, I also used a plastic "cock" ring, which is placed on the penis as close to the body as possible. This ring helps to keep the blood from leaving the penis, therefore keeping my hard penis "hard." When I walked out of the bathroom after preparing, I had the hard-on of a twenty-year-old man. Here I was at the ages of sixty-nine to seventy-four, having the best sex of my life, and I believe that if you questioned Elia she would admit feeling the same way. In fact, Elia tried many times to have us get together for an evening prior to our regular get-together, but I said no. We had one of those rare match-ups that I believe was extra pleasurable over a long period because we didn't have any extraneous pressures that one has in a normal girlfriend-boyfriend relationship.

The relationship ended when I moved to the Northwest. Did I miss my Friday sessions? Not did I only miss those wonderful times, but I knew that it was the end of the road for me. I knew that I would never, at my age, find a partner that would arouse me as Elia did, nor would I be fortunate to find someone who would be willing and happy to have such a scheduled and yet limited relationship. Time for me to apply:

DON'T BE SAD. BE GLAD FOR WHAT YOU HAD!

P.S. Unbelievable. This book is about marijuana, and here I have told you about my greatest sexual experiences, and I didn't even mention it. Believe me, every other Friday morning as I was injecting, I was also inhaling my grass. Probably the most rewarding application of the cannabis drug!

DAY 34: TIGER GOLF

The *Seattle Times* Sudoku is a six-star problem in the Saturday mornings paper. I solved it fairly quickly this morning. I have spent a great deal of time yesterday and today viewing the British Open contested at the Old Course at St. Andrews in Scotland. It is celebrating 150 years of existence as a British Open course. As usual, the weather usually wins during the four days of the tournament at this site. That is a big part of my joy in watching this tournament for so many hours. The winds were so strong (over 40 mph) that play was suspended for two hours. I believe the average golfers, like me, enjoy watching these super golfers, the world's finest, struggling. I don't have a favorite player that I root for; I usually enjoy them all. Of course, Tiger is one who I pay extra attention to. Since his recent personal problems, he has not been playing up to his previous excellence.

Today his putting was giving him fits. I don't remember which hole it was, but he missed a very short putt. As he walked off the green, I could hear him muttering, in anger, very blasphemous words. Because I was listening with headphones, I might have picked up on what he said better than most listeners. I can't wait to see if the reporters jump on this occurrence because I thought he said over and over, "FUCK! FUCK!" among other angry utterances.

Possibly prior to the telecast, the producers put together a wonderful two-minute presentation related to the "pot" bunkers on this St. Andrews golf course. I am going to try to find the words, which were very fitting and descriptive of the problems encountered when "dropping in on them." If I do find them, I will email them to my friend Ken and to my old golf club, El Cariso in Southern California. I know they will appreciate them.

Not today but soon, I am going to spend some time in this diary going into some detail of my childhood because I believe it is a factor in my addictions.

DAY 35: LEGALIZATION

The British Open is over. I spent many hours in front of my TV and enjoyed every moment. I must tell you that viewing the open on a forty-two-inch beautiful color TV is more than enjoyable; it is exciting. I cannot help myself, even with my poor memory, to think back to the first telecasts of the British Open from Europe. I don't remember the year, but I do remember it was in black and white and the TV coverage was only for the last four holes. At that time, it was still exciting—for, whoever thought that we would be watching the event live? I am not a great fan of the British Open when it is played at the Old Course at St. Andrews. Of course, I appreciate the magnificent history associated with this venue for the British Open, which moves to other courses a number of times before it returns there. I feel two negative aspects of play on that course. One is related to the rapid change in the weather elements. To me, the luck of the draw related to one's tee times very strongly affects a player's course elements, such as high wind, rain, and even cold weather. This can happen on any golf course, but I believe it is much more pronounced at St. Andrews. The other criticism is about the relative weight of one's putting abilities to the other aspects of their game. Most modern professional golfers have no problems with the driving aspects of their game on this course. So much of their success is related to their putting talents. Too much I think. Anyway it is over for this year, and I did get my kicks out of the tournament.

In today's *Sunday Seattle Times* ed-ops page, there was an article by Leonard Pitts Jr., a syndicated columnist, titled, "All Puffed Up over Marijuana." The story was about the recently declared support of an initiative that would decriminalize the use and possession of marijuana written by Alice Huffman, president of the California Conference of the NAACP. Huffman sees it as a civil rights issue. As she states, there are "four times" as many white drug users (me included) as black ones, and yet, blacks represent better than half those in state prison on drug charges. In some states, black men are jailed at a rate fifty times higher than whites. My feeling agrees with the needed legalization of marijuana but for many additional reasons. Before I enumerate my thoughts, I must tell you that any changes in laws affecting the potential income of people employed in relation to the old law is very, very strongly resisted by those people. This is true whether it is health reform, new banking changes, immigration, etc. Legalization of marijuana would certainly reduce the number of inmates in our prisons, thereby reducing the number of prison personnel making their living guarding them. I understand that the prison employees have one of the most powerful unions in the country. The legalization would reduce the number of law enforcers presently employed to prevent marijuana sales and usage.

The legalization of marijuana could not only save a great deal of funding necessary and presently spent to prevent marijuana cultivation and commerce; it would also provide a new federal income from taxing it similarly as alcohol and cigarettes. Portions of these savings could be used to conduct tests related to the beneficial and the harmful aspects of its use. It is unbelievable and ridiculous to me that alcohol, a drug for which there is a thousand times more negative effect to individuals' health per documented data and therefore costly to our culture, is legal while marijuana remains illegal for most users. There will be very strong opposition to this marijuana legalization by all in the liquor culture, greater with those who make their living from alcohol production or sales than those who use this drug. I believe there will be a tremendous exodus from alcohol users for whom marijuana will be their new drug favorite.

Other humans take drugs just as I do because they make them feel better than before taking them. And they will continue to take them, somewhat controlled by the pain/pleasure principle. It's been stated many times. You cannot legislate laws that jail or punish people for wanting what they want. It is definitely time to change.

DAY 36: HODGEPODGE

Bad start today. Did not sleep well. Am very nervous about the stock market. Overate. Only good feeling is about exercise. I am looking forward to going to the gym and starting a fast today. I have been lazy with regard to what I have been putting into my mouth. There will be no interruptions this week, and I will spend more time on this diary.

This week will be a good test as the need for a relaxation hit becomes stronger and stronger. I did not think of my drug use as a means of escape. Over the years of smoking shit, I felt it made me feel good, and thus I smoked it. I didn't feel that I was escaping from something. But now it is different. I am glad that I got started on this diary because I know if I were not involved, I definitely would be smoking right now. I am not, and I will not lie to myself or you. If I have any at all, I will either drop this book or let you know of my infidelity.

After I come home from the gym, I will try to get some rest and then spend some good time with the diary. I did very well with Suduko this morning, but you and I both know that Monday's puzzles are very easy. I also finished, yes, I said I finished, the *Sunday Seattle Times* crossword in my first attempt. It felt good to produce good results on my solving efforts.

DAY 37: CHILDHOOD FACTOR

Does your early upbringing have any bearing on your becoming an addict? If your parent or parents were addicts, would that increase or decrease your chances of becoming an addict?

I don't have the answers to these questions. I can only describe my parents and my upbringing. You can draw your own conclusions from the information that I am going to provide to you.

My father, Leopold Frederic Sielsch, was born in eastern Germany where the border between countries changed often. He had two sisters and a brother. My father came to this country when he was in his early twenties. He settled in the Philadelphia, Pennsylvania, area. I know not of his occupation in those first years in the USA. He spoke English without an accent. He met my mother, Hildegarde Johanna Rudelt, at some type of German club. She was ten years younger than he and also spoke English without an accent. My mother was born in Germany, I believe near the town of Cologne, and came to this country at age fifteen. She and her father and mother settled in Philadelphia upon arriving here.

A common occurrence between young men and woman of those times, in which there were very few pregnancy protection devices, was unprotected intercourse, resulting in pregnancies. This happened to my parents and resulted in a back and forth, in and out, of being together both before and after I was born. Apparently, my mother's father was employed as a superintendent in charge of the operation and maintenance of Full Fashioned Hosiery Machines in a company located in Germantown, Pennsylvania. Because of my grandfather's position in the hosiery (woman's stockings) manufacturing business, he apparently was able to obtain work for my father as a hosiery machine operator. Remember this was the early thirties in the depression when jobs were difficult to find, much yet get. Our family lived in the outskirts of Philadelphia until we moved to New Jersey when I was about five years old. After two years in New Jersey, we moved to Reading, Pennsylvania, where I would live until I was twenty-five years old. My father and mother opened a bar and rooming house shortly after our arrival in this town. Prior to this bar business, my mother was a stay-at-home wife and mother. But then and for the next ten years, from my age of seven to seventeen, my sister and I spent very little time with our parents. They were occupied from early morning to very late at night in this bar business. This bar business and another when we moved prevented us from really getting to know our parents. My sister, Martha, and I were on our own most of the time, but our fear of our father kept us in line and out of trouble. We rarely had dinner as a family and usually ate with the boarders, which I didn't like, but we had no choice. After about two years at this bar, we moved, when I was age nine, to a bar in the downtown area of Reading. We no longer had boarders, but still we spent very little time with our parents because of their long working hours.

The bar itself and the bar's dining room were on the first floor, and our living quarters were upstairs. I might have mentioned earlier that I had my own bedroom, which I enjoyed even though it was small and was situated above the bar's jukebox on the first floor. So again, my sister and I had great freedom to be out on the streets, which were much safer in those days than they are now. I had many little jobs that produced a small amount of income for me. I delivered papers; I cut lawns; I shoveled snow. These were common activities for young boys during those times. I always walked to school, and so did Martha. After grade school, I went to junior high school at Southern Junior High School, a mere three-block walk from our bar.

During my grade school years, I did not get to know my father as a father but more as a warden, keeping me behaving and having me get home in the evening at nine o'clock at the latest, even during my high school years. My father was a stern man who did not laugh a great deal. I never hugged my father, but I was never abused, just frightened and spanked for misbehaving. It was during the years, about ten, living at this bar called the Washington Inn, that I rarely saw my father without a cigarette in his hand. He smoked two to three packs of Lucky Strike cigarettes every day. And I mean he smoked them, those cigs spent very little time in an ashtray. His fingers, with which he usually held them, were yellowish brown, a coloring that was obvious and so strong that apparently it was very difficult to remove. As I grew, I was much more aware of my father's drinking habits. Although he drank heavily, in my estimation a fifth of cheap booze a day, it did not affect his speech or his walking. It became a medicine that enabled him to deal with the aggravations and the required social intercourse with the bar's patrons. He never should have been in this type of occupation. He definitely was not a conversationalist or even a friendly person. No wonder he drank so heavily. My mother, Hilda, did not drink to excess and was a very social person who enjoyed conversations with the patrons. She smoked very little and somehow handled the difficult responsibilities of running a working people's bar, part of every day by herself, faced with rude and crude alcoholic patrons. She was a hard-working woman. From time to time, my parents would decide to offer food in our bar in an attempt to improve the business income. It varied from lunches consisting primarily of sandwiches to periods with a fuller lunchtime menu and dinner. During those times, we would have additional help in the kitchen. The helper quite often was my aunt who did not speak English well.

My mother was loving, and we did hug, not often, but she did give me the feeling of being loved. As in many families with a son and a daughter, the father gave more attention and care to the daughter while the mother babied the son. My father was a stern person. Most of my German relatives and German men that I met and knew as a child and as a young man were also stern but not nearly as much as my father. German men of that time did not laugh much. This characteristic was so prevalent in all I ever met except one. That one was the father of my seashore neighbor, Lynn, who was exactly my age. About six months ago, I emailed her and posed some questions to her about her father. I told her of my findings regarding German men and that her father, Jack, was by far the exception. He was very social, laughed a lot, and always seemed to greet you with a big smile. How was he at home, Lynn? She emailed with glowing compliments for her father. She confirmed my observations plus. Interestingly, her mother was much more subdued and not nearly as gregarious as her father. My father—you will notice I never call him my dad—enjoyed hunting. He did take me hunting with him a few times, furnishing me with a 12-gauge shotgun, an oldie with no safety. We never had a dog until we were out of the bar business when I was seventeen and out of high school. We had two dogs, both hunting dogs. The first was an English setter that was followed by an Irish setter. The only other activity during which I remember spending time alone with my father was the period in which I was learning to drive. I had a learner's permit, and my father accompanied me in his 1937 Chevrolet sedan, which he bought new and drove until he died. But this was not exactly a pleasant learning experience. My father was not very patient, and so extra pressure was upon me during this training activity. But fortunately, I passed the driving test on my first attempt. Had I failed, I am sure not only would I have gotten an angry and disappointed response but also a renewing of training would have been really unpleasant. Lucky me, I passed.

One other important characteristic my father exhibited, big time. STUBBORNESS! Two incidents come to mind. One day the family was planning a short sixty-mile drive to a relative's farm. My father and I had a discussion as to the direction of this town we were going to visit. During this discussion, we had a very strong argument and were in total disagreement as to the compass direction we had to drive. I was sure I was correct, but he was vehement in his choice of direction. So what did I do? I went to look for a map and when I found it, there was no doubt. I was correct, and he was totally wrong. The map proved it. Then I made a big mistake. I should have been satisfied that I had proof of my assertion. But no, I took the map and opened it wide on the table and called my father to take a look. He was angry, very angry, apparently because I had the audacity to dispute his words. He took his arm and without even looking at the open map, swept it off the table, berated me, and that was that.

My other memory was related to one other activity that gave him some pleasant times. It was playing a card game called pinochle, which can be played with two or three or four players. On very slack days in the bar, he might join in a friendly game with some of his patrons. This incident that I write of occurred after we were out of the bar business. At the time, I was a good player and trounced my father badly. He was really upset in a fashion similar to the map incident. He threw the cards to the floor, made some nasty remark, and we never played pinochle together again, thank goodness.

My father was not a clean man. He did not bathe nearly enough. As I grew older and became more aware of his habits, I wondered how my mother could sleep with him. He also did not take care of his teeth. They were in terrible condition. Also my parents never taught that a daily brushing of our teeth was required to maintain them. And to make things worse with all of the freedom I had, I ate too much sweet sugary candy that I now am sure sat in my teeth for days. The result was horrible lifetime teeth problems, which I will not get into at this time.

One other mentionable item regarding my parents is that I never saw either of them reading a book. Ever. I know they were hardworking and busy, but still when I think back on it, I can only attribute my love affair with book reading to my teachers. This avid development to learn, especially from books, continues to this day. For whatever reasons, starting with my early days of reading books, almost every book that I chose to read was non-fiction. Somewhere along the way, I became somewhat obsessed with learning something new every day. I was a subscriber to *Scientific American* for over twenty-five years until every subject became so complex and deep that it was impossible to comprehend many of the writings in this journal. I will somewhere in this diary also tell you of my religious affiliations, none at the present but baptized and confirmed in the Lutheran faith backed up by three years in catechetical classes (forced upon me by my father who never even attended any church services).

I realize that I could write a book about my parents and my early years. But, as I said earlier, I was not abused or beaten or exposed to unethical, racial, or radical religious ideas. I always felt that when becoming an adult one should be able to assess one's early years and decide the directions and beliefs to guide one's own choices. I don't know as I am not a psychologist or psychiatrist capable of relating my addictive behavior at present to my upbringing. I do know from personal experience, living with a partner, that early strong and dedicated religious training can cause much mental conflict later in life. I am sure that abused children also must suffer the consequences resulting from aberrant early experiences.

DAY 38: PINBALL TILT

I know that without my writing this diary I would have indulged myself by now and in addition the likelihood of a successful withdrawal would have been more difficult if I had a live-in partner.

Why didn't I become an addicted alcoholic? I had every opportunity to imbibe all types of alcohol or beer at a very young age. I experimented. On Sundays, our Washington Inn was closed so my parents usually didn't arise until noon, giving me the opportunity to test some of the many booze bottles on the shelf. Over time, I tried most of them, not in volume enough to become intoxicated but enough to know if I liked the taste. Taste mattered to me, and at that young age, probably between twelve and fourteen, most liquor was distasteful.

As a small aside, we had a jukebox in our bar, and we also had a pinball machine. I loved it, but my father never allowed me to play with it. Can you guess? On Sunday mornings, I would go in the drawer in the bar that contained a sizeable quantity of slugs. These were utilized to provide a free game for our patrons if the machine functioned improperly and the customer lost his nickel, yes, nickels for the juke and the pinball. My parents' bedroom was upstairs in the rear, a long distance from the bar. The pinball games of those days were not as noisy as they are today. Sometimes both my parents would go out on a Sunday, and that was my real opportunity to get some experience with the game. I learned a few tricks that I could apply on the machine at the neighborhood's local soda and candy hangout, which paid a nickel for each earned game. Every one who has ever played a pinball machine knows.

For those of you who haven't had that fun experience as a young person or old person, I will explain. First of all, I would guess the name pinball was formed from the fact that the machine had various *pins* that were struck or rolled over by the *ball*. Makes sense then to call the device a *pinball* machine. To play a game, you placed a nickel in a slot that it fitted snugly and pushed it forward. When it came back without the nickel, you were supplied with five metal, probably chromed, balls, about an inch in diameter. At your end of the machine where you had inserted your nickel, there was a rod that when pushed would lift one of those five shiny balls to a position ready to be projected into the workings of the machine. You worked a spring-loaded mechanism, usually on the right side so you had to use your right hand to activate this mechanism, which would send the ball rolling up and into the machine. Our bar changed machines often so that our patrons would not get bored playing the same old machine. Each machine was usually designed and laid out with pins or slots that gave high scores when the rolling ball contacted them. So the idea was to sense the amount of spring tension that was required to project the ball in position to bump or slide through special slots, both usually well lit and prominent as to their great value in scoring.

The machine was not level. It was solidly placed on the floor at a slight angle so that a ball projected would actually be rolling up a slight incline, and when it reached the top of the entryway, gravity would cause the ball to return downward to where it would eventually fall into its original resting place. Of course, on its travels down the incline, it would strike various bumpers, which would score points that were accumulated and displayed on the machine. Also, the ball could travel through various passageways, containing spring-loaded slots that also scored points to be displayed and accumulated with previous scorings. The object of the game was to accumulate a high enough score to obtain a free game. After one ball had completed its gravity-driven roll to the original resting place, the player could now push the rod to bring the second ball into position. Having seen the results of the first ball's trajectory, the player would now apply a spring load that would result in more scoring than the first ball.

This process was repeated for all five balls, and with each ball, the player would try to improve his touch on the spring projecting the ball, thereby increasing his scoring enough to get some free games.

Most players, especially experienced gamers, after projecting the ball on its way, would place their hands on the left and right side of the machine in such a manner to give them the ability to slightly move the machine in an attempt to affect the rolling ball. The purpose of this maneuvering was to alter the ball's rolling in ways that would accomplish a number of desirable alterations. The most important was to attempt to keep the ball from reaching its final destination. Keep the ball in play as long as possible, thereby continually adding points to your total score. Or slightly move the machine with your hands to enter or bump those slots or bumpers giving very high scores.

Now I am going to explain the word that appears on the machine that makes the player very angry, so much so that spectators watching the player may be exposed to some swear words from the player. What is that word that could make the player so unhappy that he shouts and carries on badly? **TILT** is the word. Yes, the four letter word **TILT** appearing on the machine means that the player, in attempting to control the path of the ball using his hands, has exceeded the allowable amount of agitation accepted by the machine's tilt limits. Now why does this four-letter word anger the player so much? The machine stops functioning. No more scoring. But even worse—the player's remaining balls cannot be used. The game is over, and if the upset player wants to play another game, he must put in another nickel. Of course, if the player has done well in previous plays and has earned some free plays, he need not put a nickel in, just use one of his free plays for the next game.

What is the mechanism that detects the motion caused by the player's pushing that exceeds the allowable amount of movement, thereby tilting the game? Often I had the opportunity to be present when the nickels the machine had collected over a period of time were withdrawn. After all, this was the incentive for having the machine in the bar in the first place, to make money. In order to remove the mass of nickels, the machine's cover had to be lifted and maintained in a position enabling the machine's owner to remove his loot. Aha! At these times, the interior workings of the machine were visible.

And I was all eyes for this was my chance to understand the working of the most important mechanism to me, the **TILT** mechanism. All of the pinball machines that I had the opportunity to see inside had the same tilt mechanism.

What was this mechanism that angered the players? First of all, it was a very simple device consisting of a ring of metal approximately one inch in diameter, fastened securely. The other part was a thin one-eighth-inch diameter rod, hanging freely above and through the one-inch cylinder but steadied by the force of gravity. These two parts were connected electrically to the machine parts that would stop the play and cause the **TILT** sign to appear. When the connection between these two parts was open, the pinball machine functioned normally. However when the machine was excessively pushed and shoved in the player's efforts to make the ball move in the direction he desired, the hanging rod swaying from the player's efforts touched the circular ring, completing the tilt circuit. Bingo! Up goes the **TILT** sign, and the machine shuts down while the angry player is shouting, "I didn't push it enough to tilt it. There's something wrong with this lousy machine." I knew very well how this mechanism operated, and having this knowledge gave me a technique that would enable me to "beat" many of these pinball machines.

The best way to roll up a high score was to keep the ball from rolling through a pin-type scoring slot and have it roll slightly forward, causing a score, and then slightly backward (from the force of the pin mechanism) then forward and backward, etc., racking up an unbelievably high score, resulting in many free games. How would I accomplish this masterful method of getting free games? Is it accomplished by my shoves and pushes when the ball is in the pin slot? No. Now remember that the machine is set on an incline causing the ball to roll in the direction of the bottom of the machine where the ball magazine is located. When it is rolling down and enters one of the pin type scoring slots, the gravity force pulls it through after scoring from the pin movement. The way to cause the ball to perform its back-and-forth pin-slot action is to reduce the incline, which reduces the pull of gravity, enabling the back-forth scoring so desired. The way to reduce the incline and therefore lessen the gravitational effect is to carefully put the machine's front legs onto the tops of your shoes. Now this is an extremely sensitive operation requiring a tender touch. Can you visualize that as you raise the machine to put it on your feet, the rod in the tilt mechanism is heading toward a connection with the cylinder that surrounds it? If you raise it too high, then contact will be made, and boom—**TILT** occurs. If you raise it in a clumsy fashion, the rod will assuredly make contact with the cylinder surrounding it. The key is to raise very, very gently the machine to your toe tops. Now on most pinball machines, after you have projected the ball, it—or the next ball or the next ball, you have five tries—will enter one of the pin-type scoring slots and perform as described above, rolling back and forth, scoring points forever, eventually enough to give you a large quantity of free games. This was an easy technique to apply in my bar when I was alone. But to pull this stunt in the local watering hole required the assistance of a lookout for the proprietor, warning of his coming in our direction—or the assistance of a crowd about the machine, thereby hiding what was going on. Not an easy task. But let us say we got forty free games; the proprietor paid us a nickel a game, a total of two dollars, which wasn't peanuts for a twelve-year-old at that time.

Enough of the pinball game except for two more illegal methods to obtain free plays. Number one was the "slugs," which I had explained earlier. Just insert the slug in place of the nickel; however, the risk was that some machines not only rejected the slug but caused the money input mechanism to jam. Better get out of there fast. One other technique to obtain free games was to use the thin long metal rod from a lady's girdle of those times. Remove that rod from the girdle, hide it on your body, and then when the proprietor was busy, put the rod under the coin input mechanism. Then push that mechanism as though you had a nickel coin in it and usually the effort would result in the machine being fooled, and you get to play without inserting your nickel. Oh, the things we did when we were kids!

My father also was a heavy cigarette smoker so there were always cigs about, making it easy for me to try some. But I didn't. I think there were two basic reasons I didn't even once test a smoke. One, probably the strongest, was the fear that my father would be very unhappy with me, resulting in some type of capital punishment. Fear is the workhorse that prevented me from many exploratory adventures. Reason two was an experience I had with my grandfather a few years earlier. I was curious about his smoking, which was cigars. One day I bugged him about his stogies, and so to shut me up, he offered me a few puffs. It was awful. I thought at the time—my age was about eleven—how could anyone do this. Although I became an addicted smoker later, I never liked cigars. During one period when I was trying to quit my cigarette addiction, I tried pipes. I liked the tastes of different tobaccos, but I was inhaling just the same as I was with cigs. In addition, I had holes in my shirts and pants from falling embers. Plus it was an extra drag to have to take the junk with you everywhere you went, the pipe had to be relit quite often, and it was difficult to smoke on the golf course. I believe my pipe experience lasted maybe eight months.

DAY 39: ALCOHOL

As the days pass, it is not getting easier to deny myself that good feeling I know I will receive if I light up. Again, I repeat that the writing exercise of this diary and its already significant investment of time and work, typing and writing, is a strong incentive to continue to avoid weed. I know it would be much easier to withdraw if I started smoking cigarettes again, but I feel the cigarette habit is worse for your health than smoking marijuana. So I will keep on typing and writing and writing and typing.

I have released some of the tension that was causing me to consider ending this attempt to quit my habit. I sold, at a loss, a good portion of my stock portfolio. This meant that all of the realized gains that I had made prior to this time were more than offset by these realized losses. However, my outlook is that the market is in a slow spiral downward and will not recover in a strong positive way for years. Unfortunately, I have two stocks that if I sold them today the loss would be very substantial. I have decided to keep these, one of which is a biotech stock, which has a product that has been patented but has not shown up well enough in the FDA testing cycles to gain acceptance. It is still alive, and I have thought for months now that another larger biotech company would purchase this company. So far, it hasn't happened. The company has reduced its personnel and has enough funds to last until 2011. It is trading at its lowest value in its history at the present time, and unless something happens either with the FDA or an acquisition, it will probably go bankrupt.

The other stock is a large shipping company whose value has dropped because of the decrease in global activities during these trying times. This stock will make it back to the price at which I purchased it, but it may take more than a year.

It is my belief that we are headed for a much longer economic recovery than many of us thought initially. I believe the spurt of stock market increases in mid 2009 until May of 2010 occurred because of federal stimulus of various kinds. This socialistic kind of government operation cannot go on forever. We are no different from Greece or Spain or any other country that has been outspending its income. The USA and other countries have been living beyond our means for too long. The true way to correct this situation is to spend less, meaning we all will have to give up some things for a number of years. Unfortunately, for savers such as me, another technique to resolve our huge debt problem is to print lots of money, creating an inflationary period of uncertain economic times. Many investors are into gold, which they feel will protect them from the difficulties coming soon. At any rate, my tension has abated some, primarily because being on the fence is very tense and making decisions reduces the tension. But so would a few hits!

Now I went through some of my growing-up history and gave you some information about my parents and how we lived. My father was an alcoholic and an addicted smoker. I did not become an alcoholic. I am not even a good social drinker, and I believe I can tell you why.

I told you about my sampling of different alcoholic drinks in my youth. I never really got into some serious drinking until I was out of high school. I had peer pressure to drink from many of my friends. So I drank. Fortunately, I too often became very ill from booze. My first very negative experience was at age seventeen when I drank too much wine. I will never forget the consequences of that overindulgence. Up to that time, I had never felt the awful sense of the world spinning and my inability to make it stop and those heaves of what felt like everything I had eaten or drunk for days. And that wasn't the worst part—the dry heaves when there was no more to throw up. It was very bad, a new experience for me that I resolved would not happen again. But it did, but never as severely as that first time. Although I became ill from booze during my drinking days,

I never again felt that terribly frightening feeling of the world spinning out of control. Thank goodness for that. The only time I ever again had similar ill feelings that way, but even worse, was a vertigo experience I had in my forties. As I aged, I drank less, and even during my periods being employed in a sales position where part of my necessary duties was to entertain clients, I learned how to cope. My alcoholic drug of choice for many years of entertaining was Compari tall with lime, which I sipped. My clients would quite often have three martinis during a one-hour lunch, then return to work. I don't know how they did it; I couldn't.

I want to write about my general living situation in the town of Lynnwood, which is about fifteen miles north of the biggest city in the state of Washington, namely, Seattle. You must remember that prior to moving here I lived in Southern California for fifty years; the majority of those years and the last place was in Hollywood.

DAY 40: HODGEPODGE

I believe I am facing the first major hurdle in this withdrawal effort. It is the difficulty I am having sleeping. It is now, as I write this, one twenty in the morning. I went to bed at ten, woke at eleven thirty, came to the computer and wrote a letter to Nancy Lublin, who titled her book about the operation of not-for-profit organizations *Zilch: The Power of Zero in Business*, finished that letter, and went back to bed at twelve thirty, and here I am back at the computer. As noted above, it is now one twenty.

Starting this moment, I will not drink coffee for a week, and that includes decaf. If I find my sleeping improves, I will dump all the coffee I have in my condo. I really believe that the pot that I smoked every evening was a great help in sleeping.

Water will be my substitute for evening liquid. Maybe I should try some wine at night. *Hold on, Leo; don't panic. Wait to see what happens when you remove coffee from your liquid intake.*

I did not consume any coffee today. The time is ten at night, and I am about to turn in. I did drink tea today, but it was decaf. I do not feel sleepy, but I am going to bed by eleven. I will report on my sleep tomorrow.

DAY 41: PATIENCE

Same sleep pattern seems to prevail no matter what I drink. Although I must admit taking naps has become easier to do. They are usually about a half hour long.

This is a Friday, and that is Sudoku five-star today. Good start. I finished the five-star in the *USA Today* on the first try. Unfortunately, I cannot say the same for the *Seattle Times* Sudoku. I am struggling on that one, but I'll get it, I'm sure.

I read a story the other day that said marijuana may be helpful in preventing Alzheimer's disease. Hard for me to believe, but all comments or stories of this nature are pure conjectures; there is no testing data that I can find backing up those type of favorable comments. Must be a user hoping to help it become legal as soon as possible. These thoughts are the exact opposite of that which I am inclined to toss about. From all that I have written to this point in my diary, one of my main focuses is the problem potentially caused by prolonged daily use. Alzheimer's, to me, would seem a most likely result of long-term usage. However, don't get me wrong. Just because I think that is possible, I am hoping that the evidence of my crude measuring abilities points to no effect or even a positive effect. Too early to tell.

Tomorrow will be a good test of my successes to date in my withdrawal plan. I am having a pizza and spinach salad evening with my son Vic, daughter-in-law, Donna, and two young friends who are heavy users. I will offer my stuff, and it will be smoked, and

I resolve not to indulge. Not even one hit because I am afraid that is all I need to start me off. Again, I know that the writing of this diary keeps me from smoking and keeps me honest! It is a point I will highlight over and over to those long-term addicts who are desirous of quitting marijuana.

DAY 42: TV WEED

Yes, everyone had a nice time, and all were entertained by Tweeter. For the first time, we understood his talking. What did he say? All things that I repeated many, many times like, "I love you" and "pretty boy" and "spin the wheel." He got on the finger of everyone, and all enjoyed, including Tweeter. Did I join the grass smoking? No! Did I want to? Yes, but it was not difficult to resist.

I just ordered the first year of the TV show *Weed*, which Vic and his wife and our guests watch and rave about. They are saying it is as good as *The Sopranos* but with better music. I am looking forward to watching because I really enjoyed *The Sopranos*.

There is no doubt in my mind that if I weren't involved with this diary I would be smoking pot. I hope that all readers of this diary who are long-term users and want to quit have a strong motivator; otherwise they won't make it. I haven't made it yet myself, but I do feel confident that I will. There seems to be some news about marijuana in the papers or on the TV every day. It usually goes from medical marijuana to the capture of some large amount.

A number of subjects related to marijuana I have not yet written about. The using of the drug marijuana leads to using what most people feel are the more serious drugs, such as opiates and amphetamines. Did I ever try either of those drugs? No, I did not. There are a couple of reasons that I never got involved with those drugs during my forty years of smoking pot. I am a control freak. Anything that I would smoke or take by mouth that I had read or been told would result in "out of your mind" feelings frightened me so much that I would not even try them. That was one of the main factors about my marijuana use for so many years; I always felt in control. Now don't get me wrong. I did not like driving while loaded. That doesn't mean that I didn't do it; I'm just telling you that I would avoid it whenever possible, but there were times that it was unavoidable, such as times when you smoked away from your home, meaning you eventually had to drive home, loaded or not. I was one of those who became paranoid when driving loaded and, in some ways, a better driver when loaded because I did not speed or take any risky moves. I drove further behind the car in front of me. But even though I could do it, driving while loaded, I didn't like it and avoided it whenever possible. I also didn't like being a passenger in a car driven by someone who was loaded unless I knew the person very well and knew of his or her capabilities and actions while loaded.

I tried cocaine, the powder variety, once or twice. Very small amounts that didn't do much for me. I never tried amphetamines because I took dope to relax, not to be hyped up. I was that way—relaxed—before I used a drug, a somewhat normal disposition for me. As I told you earlier, I used grass to cool me down and not be so serious and so overly concerned that social intercourse was a waste of good time. One time, on the golf course, my foursome got into a discussion related to moving to other (harsher and more dangerous) drugs as a result of smoking pot. Two of the foursome smoked pot, my friend Jim and I, and neither of us felt that smoking grass would lead to worse addictions. We smoked on the course but very discreetly. However, on this discussion day, one member of our group became very upset with our espousing the safeties associated with our habit. He had a son that had gone on to other drugs and apparently caused major problems in his family. He was so vehement that we could not continue the discussion. Various pills and drugs at the high school age were just not available when I went to high school, and even in college (WPI), I never ran into them. Who knows what I might have tried had they been available? I never even knew what marijuana was when I was in high school and college. That might have been a good thing.

Peer pressure when you are young is mighty powerful. I did some drinking during my late teens. Stupid, really, because I didn't enjoy booze. For one thing, when I drank too much, I got sick as a dog. Oh, how I remember those incidents. One night I remember sleeping in the snow in the wee hours of the morning. Another night I came home feeling terrible and wound up with both car doors open and me stretched out, feet out one side and my head the other side, heaving until I thought I would die. Even though I had numerous experiences of this kind, I still found myself getting drunk and sick a few times in my thirties, joining in when I shouldn't have. What a dummy! I must admit that my working career involved many social occasions where alcohol was the party kicks, but I had learned my lesson well. I drank but sipped, and the slightest feeling of inebriation caused me to back off big time. Many occasions, I was entertaining customers so my tasks were to see that they enjoyed themselves and to take care of them. I often thought that I was fortunate to not have become an alcoholic because booze, even free booze, was available to me for many years.

In 2008, I read a newspaper article that wrote about a herbal leaf that gives you a marijuana-type feeling and was legal although a number of states were considering making it illegal. I don't remember the exact name, it might have been "salvia," and I purchased a starter pack on the Internet. It was not expensive. The starter pack consisted of one ounce of dried salvia foliage and a small packet of 5x and 10x powder extracts. Now remember I had been smoking weed for almost forty years at that time, always hiding and being secretive. The thought that I could get a high like that of grass and not have to worry about its legality, both buying and using it, was terrific. Sounded great to me.

So I get this stuff in the mail, and it looks exactly like the picture on the site where I purchased it. So not long after I received it, I tried the leaf, which I thought would be much milder than the powder. I put a small amount into my pipe, took a puff or two, and waited for a reaction. After a few minutes, the amount of time a good hit of grass would have given me a high, I felt very little effect from this leaf. I noticed only that it made me lean a little forward when walking. Even that effect lasted only a few minutes. So as far as I was concerned, this stuff was a scam and I wasted my twenty-five or thirty dollars or whatever it was. I put the stuff away and forgot about it.

About three months later, I was in an experimental mood and low on the good stuff. *Hey Leo, this might be a good time to try the powder from that scam; maybe you'll get something out of the concentrated portion.* So I opened the little pack of a dark brown powder and put some into my pipe. I took two big hits and thought it was kind of harsh tasting. One half minute later, it happened. Wow and again wow! I had never in all my years of smoking shit ever, ever felt what I felt then. It was more than a feeling; it was the most frightening experience I ever had. I was in my bedroom and the hallway from it leads straight to the exit door. Even today I don't like thinking about what happened next.

THE HOUSE WAS LEAVING OUR PLANET EARTH. I RAN TO THE DOOR TO ESCAPE BECAUSE THIS HOUSE WAS LEAVING PLANET EARTH.

I definitely was out of my mind. I must have been yelling because when I got outside and sat down on the steps, the lady tenant from the apartment above came down the steps and asked if I needed help. I just wanted it to end. I sat on those steps and told her I was okay. I was alert enough to be embarrassed and wondering what she thought about me. Again, I tell you I don't remember yelling, but I must have, to have brought her down the steps and for her to offer assistance. I was afraid to get up. I sat there, and I was sweating on a cold day. I don't know how long I sat on those steps for time was a mystery. Finally, I went back into the apartment, which, thank goodness, had not left planet earth. I drank some water and sat. I was still very frightened that the feeling might return. I called my son and my daughter-in-law and asked them to come right away. I needed them right now. In the two years since I had moved here, close to where they lived, I never had asked their help in this manner. I sat, still shook up, and waited for them to arrive. *God, where are they?*

While I was waiting, still dazed, I worried that it was not over. It could start again. I didn't get up; I sat still. Then I thought about the tenants from above, the nice Asian lady who had come to see if I needed help. I must have yelled, but I don't remember. Who else heard me? Fortunately, it was a weekday late afternoon and not a weekend.

Finally, they were here, but by then it was over. I thanked them for coming and then told them the story of what had happened. They listened and listened for I had never experienced anything like this. I, for some reason or other, wanted them to know what I had gone through. Of course, they said I should have some water. Any type of accident, they would say, "C'mon, drink some water." Is that the correct thing to do, drink water? Well, I think it relaxes both parties, the injured and the helpers. They soon left, feeling that I was OK and didn't need them any longer. It was true; I was OK, but I still sat around for another hour or two and then quickly disposed of the "devil" leaf and powder. So that was my "out of this world" experience. I read that there are people who do this kind of thing often; apparently they enjoy their trips into space.

It must have been fifteen years earlier that I attended a "Good Earth" type of convention in San Diego where one of the main speakers was Timothy Leary, a very intelligent person who was a famous pioneer in drug-induced feelings and actions. He did this experimenting with drugs and lecturing about his drug experiences for a good number of years. His presentation was very well done, and after hearing him speak, I had the opportunity to have a very short discussion. I was impressed. His behavior, manner, and speeches showed no sign of any deterioration of his abilities. Now remember this was a long time ago, way before I had my "trip" and lived to write about it.

I am tired and will try to take a short nap before I continue.

DAY 43: HODGEPODGE

Today is my son's birthday. I treated my son and his wife to dinner at the Claim Jumper restaurant, where the meals are good and large. No writing done on this day.

DAY 44: EYE EXAMS

Today I had an appointment at ten thirty to have my eyes examined. The facility is located in Seattle, about fifteen miles from my place. I often wondered, and I thought it to be true, if the doctor doing the examination can easily detect that you have been smoking grass. The next question is: does the smoking of marijuana make it more difficult to examine the user's eyes? If my memory is right, during the initial visit to any medical practitioner, one is required to fill out basic information forms—address, name, illnesses, telephone number, and such. I always tried to inform them of my drug usage at this time. In all of the years that I followed this procedure, my habit was not discussed then or ever again. I would have thought that this information would have been an integral part of a person's papers so that those performing any test or medical procedure would be aware of the client's drug habits, just as they are informed and knowledgeable of a client's medications. No doctor has ever even hinted that my marijuana consumption should cease. Who knows? Maybe they are users.

Now back to the drive to the eye medical facilities. I had not driven over thirty miles an hour for over a year. This, my first freeway trip, was a little scary. At first, I drove at fifty miles an hour (in the slow lane) with the speed limit being sixty-five miles an hour. I soon got up to sixty miles an hour and felt fairly comfortable, possibly because the traffic was light. Before I knew it, I was there. Started the examination—looking with one eye; is it better with #1 or #2? Then another row of letters. Read the smallest row that you can. On and on, never having a clue as to the measurements of my vision being good or bad. Now the drops, blinding though they are, are necessary to complete the next part of the examination. Making a long story short, my eyes are good seers and healthy besides. The drive home was a breeze. Sixty-five miles an hour right from the start.

I am not having strong yearnings for the stuff today, partly because there are no major concerns giving me small fits that I would like to dispel. I feel good without the shit. Plus I slept better yesterday and napped yesterday and today. But the important point is do I miss it? Yes, I do. Why do you think I smoked it for all those years? I enjoyed the feelings it gave me, and I am sure of the good feelings that I would get if I lit up right now. Maybe I need some of you long-term users, such as I, but with health problems definitely tied to your addiction to write a diary. Maybe I need to feel grateful that I am not having any major health problems at this time and I should definitely quit while I am ahead. So if you are an unhappy longtime user, I plan to have my email address within this diary when it is published so that you can contact me. Of course, I think about finishing my writing. What is my plan? I have not made any resolutions to quit forever. My thoughts shuffle back and forth between: I am so lucky to have had forty years of pleasure from marijuana without illness and "Don't be sad; be glad, for what you had." Or should I have a hit or two every once in a while but not overdo it? After all, there is no evidence that you will be penalized if you continue using. Testing is needed. But for now, writing this diary requires that I stay clean.

DAY 45: ADDICTION

Went to bed early and slept well. My sleep may not be more than five hours, but it is solid. And remember my naptime of one hour has to be added in, giving me six hours. If I were to accept those hours as the correct number, I'd be fine. I am not going to write about it anymore. It's boring me, and you must be tired of reading about my sleep.

What are the thoughts for today? I wonder about others, men and woman, who are addicts like me. I probably said it before, but I would be very interested in their thoughts. Do they even think about quitting? Are they having any physical problems because of their habit? Does the habit interfere with their work life? Do they smoke all day long, starting when they arise? Did they start at a very young age? And what about if they have children; how do they handle that?

I do know one couple who were users, but that was before they had a child. But I don't know the details of their smoking. I couldn't call them addicts because I wasn't with them often enough to witness their habit. Maybe as a result of this book, we all will learn more about the usage habits and the feelings this couple have about their addiction. I never felt I had an addiction probably because I never tried to quit using. So when is one's use considered an addiction? Let me look it up in the dictionary. The one that sounds reasonable to me is "persistent compulsive use of a substance known by the user to be harmful." The problem with that definition is that there is no good evidence that persistent compulsive use of marijuana is harmful. I never felt it was harmful. I think a better definition is "the daily use of marijuana that does not negatively affect the user's daily life," meaning that the usage is a habit rather than an addiction. I love ice cream, and I could eat it every day, but I know that would be harmful to my good health. Therefore, I don't have it every day. I have been somewhat addicted to various sweets over the years. At the present time, I am having a difficult time eliminating the peanut butter M&M's candies from my diet. I could eat some in the morning, at lunch, for dinner, and at bedtime. I freeze them, which makes them crunchy, to my delight. If you are using, eating, drinking, or just plain taking something into your body on a regular basis and can't stop, then you are an addict.

I found myself eating ice cream by the gallon, at times making ice cream my dinner meal or buying a full gallon in the morning, eating some later in the morning, and eating nothing but ice cream for the rest of the day. I would call that an addiction. But is it? I was eating ice cream on a regular basis, but when I moved to the state of Washington, I vowed to stop. And I did. But the craving never went away. I want it right now as I type my thoughts onto this page. It comes right down to the pleasure/pain principle. Any daily habit that gives one pleasure will be continued unless either it does not please anymore or it interferes with one's daily life. There is no physical discomfort from not eating ice cream. I would certainly call it an addiction if you felt heartburn after eating and took a medication to relieve the pain from your use. I don't get any pain from my M&M's, but I know that I am taking on calories that are not beneficial to my good health.

I have a habit of daily regular usage, which many people, including some medical people, would consider an addiction, depending upon their perception. It is coffee. I have been drinking coffee daily for over sixty years. Coffee is one of those liquids that we drink, which has available many views, some favorable and some unfavorable, about its usage. That's where the perception comes in, how you interpret those available views. During recent times, there have been articles providing favorable information, that coffee is good for the heart. Well, I certainly wasn't aware of this possibility when I started drinking coffee or in the years since. I started with coffee probably because my father drank it, and it was available everywhere. My initial taste for coffee required me to add sugar and milk. Initially, I drank it only in the morning, but as time went by and I had desk jobs, I drank it all day long and sometimes in the evening also.

Now I wrote of coffee earlier in this diary because of my sleeping difficulties and attempting to learn if coffee was the cause. I have used decaf coffee at various times during those sixty years, but mostly in the last twenty. For many years, I could drink as much regular coffee anytime of the day and go to sleep without a problem. That has changed. I give every effort to quit regular coffee after four in the afternoon, when I switch over to decaf.

I also drink tea at times, more of it in the winter than in the summer. But the four-o'clock rule applies to regular tea just the same as coffee. I believe I drink much more coffee and tea now that I live in the Northwest where the weather is much colder than in Southern California. I try to drink more water, not tap water, which I have generally avoided over the years, but the volume doesn't even come near that of coffee. Again, the pleasure/pain principle applies. Believe me, if I felt pain after drinking coffee or tea, it wouldn't take long for me to drop them from my diet. I also drink diet soda although not in great quantities. It probably isn't good for me, but again, I like it. The ideal liquid to put into your body is water. Wouldn't I like to enjoy water so much that it would be the only liquid I drink? Yes and yes. I drink lots of water in the morning at the gym but very little during the rest of the day.

Let me sum my feelings regarding the drinking of coffee, tea, or diet soda. I do not consider those habitual uses to be an addiction because I do not consider either of those items to be seriously harmful to me. But I do consider the inhaling or eating of cannabis possibly to be harmful, and therefore I consider my daily use, knowing that it could cause problems and that it is illegal, to indicate I am an addict.

I am very happy that my three children, ages fifty-one, fifty-six, and fifty-eight, do not have an addiction to drugs as I do. They have been and still are great examples of hard workers, honest in their dealings, and loving and respectful to their father. As the song goes, "Who Could Ask for Anything More?"

DAY 46: WEEDS AND FAMILY

Did you ever view a TV show and have mixed reactions? I watched *Weeds* last night, the first three episodes. I was shocked. I know it's supposed to be a comedy, but the thought that all ages of young people are going to view this show appalled me. It killed my efforts to laugh at the goings-on in *Weeds*. In my opinion, it set back the legalization of marijuana for years. It makes me feel much stronger towards legalization with strong controls to protect our children. I know that it is a comedy, but it comes off like a reality show. I was a fan of *The Sopranos*, which was not a comedy. It showed a side of our culture that exists but few of us, especially seniors, see or feel. But the children in the show were always cared for in a manner with concern for their exposure to life that they were too young to understand. In *Weeds*, the participants were not ghetto or poor families but, as in the opening, lawyers, accountants, and doctors. They resided in expensive homes in high-class neighborhoods, and it was difficult for me to remember that this was a comedy and was not to be taken seriously. It made fun of our ethics and our morals. I wonder about the demographics of the viewers of this apparently very successful show. I would venture to say that the seniors in my community are not viewing this show. The road to legalization has been lengthened and made more difficult. I can see it now—opponents of legalization using examples from *Weeds* to further their efforts to prevent legalization, not just now, but for years. It's this generation's *Reefer Madness*.

I believe that it makes my diary much more important. I had been thinking, prior to watching *Weeds*, about soliciting diaries, information, and feelings from other long-term addicts. I now feel stronger about such an activity. Just because I seem to have been fortunate not to have, so far, any major health problems that I can tie to my forty years of indulgence, doesn't mean that all users have had no health problems. We need the tests, and we need more users to come forward. I did not intend this diary to be an example of the freedom from worry of the bad effects of years of marijuana use. It is a day-to-day writing of the feelings, thoughts, and actions of a long-term addict attempting withdrawal possibly leading to total abstinence. Just like the serious consequences many have suffered from smoking cigarettes for many years, I am sure that many pot addicts have also suffered serious consequences from their habit. Or maybe the techniques for obtaining the cannabis high are a factor in the physical effects the body incurs or, more important, doesn't incur.

I would also be appreciative of any comments, test results, and or evidence from people in the medical field. At this time, I am not sure how to obtain, structure, and utilize data from addicts and/or medical experts. It is something I will think about as my withdrawal goes forward. Knowing how addicts came to be addicts is also important data and can only be gotten from addicts.

As to my yearning for a hit or two today, my thirst for weed has been somewhat quenched by viewing the show. Generally, I have been able to handle the urges to indulge myself, just a little bit. I think my recent experience will strengthen my will to withdraw. It's morning as I write these words, and I will quit writing for now.

I always felt that the greatest dangers of smoking marijuana were to the lungs and throat. So at various times during my forty years, I would experiment, usually with "loaded" chocolate chip cookies but sometimes with other techniques. There is no doubt that I could achieve a high by eating the "loaded" cookies, but the feeling was subtle and required twenty minutes to an hour before feeling anything. The rush was not there, but the feeling was good for relaxing. I also tried grinding the grass to a fine powder and placing it in tea. Same effect as with the cookies. Another technique I tried was to place the powdered marijuana in a glass with Scotch. I placed the glass in the fridge for weeks, stirring it often, but the grass never dissolved into the Scotch. Somewhere I had read that in Jamaica they had such a drink. I wonder, if I had heated the mixture, would that have made a difference? Too late now, anyway.

My sister, two years younger than I, grew up in the same bar environment that I did. She never got into weed even though I offered her a trial many times over the years. However, she did get into booze, especially during the later years when she was caring for her husband, who has Parkinson's disease. But I definitely would not define her as an addict. She would have maybe two drinks, usually vodka, at the end of the day when her hubby of fifty-some years was safely in his bed. My mother worked in the bar for all of the years that our family was in the bar business. She drank, but very little. She definitely was not an alcoholic, which was a good thing because it didn't take much liquor to change her demeanor into that of a very silly, childlike lady. The opposite of my father who could drink all day and show no signs of being affected, my mother was a different person after two or three drinks.

I was very upset when I was exposed to the childlike behavior associated with my mother's drinking. I have a scar on the palm of my right hand from an incident that occurred when I was about fourteen. My sister and I were spending our summer at my grandparents' bungalow in Surf City on Long Beach Island in New Jersey. Normally my grandparents, who resided in Philadelphia, would drive to my hometown, Reading, Pennsylvania, to pick my sister and me up for the summer vacation. We might spend some time in Philadelphia before my grandparents, my sister, and I would head for the New Jersey bungalow. During the time in Philly, I got to touch the crack in the Liberty Bell at age nine.

The routine was altered one year when my parents drove my sister and me to the seashore. They stayed for a few days and partied. On one of those party days, I was in the house watching the goings on in the yard outside. I was shamed by my mother's behavior. Even at the young age of eleven, which I was at that time, I was sensitive to the odd behavior of drunken people. After all, I had been exposed to them for four or five years by then. I became so enraged at my mom's behavior that I lost my control. I crashed my fist through a window, not thinking at all of the potential consequences of such an act. I started bleeding while my parents, who had heard the sound of the glass crashing to the ground, came rushing in to my side. I was glad in a way to have had some injury from the stupid but strong impulse to crash my hand the way I had done. My father would have given me a good and severe licking if I had survived the incident without any sign of injury. I was more frightened by the possible beating from my angry father than I was of the bleeding palm. This is an early sign, when added to all of those years of exposure to intoxicated people, of experiences that may have conditioned me to avoid the consumption of an amount of alcohol that would cause me to behave like a fool. During my late teens and twenties, I did drink. But if I consumed too much, before I could be the fool, I became very ill. This experience of heaving till I felt my insides would be outside happened a few times until I learned to be a social drinker. Good thing because my occupation in future years necessitated that I entertain customers, which most times involved liquor drinking. I never ever drank an amount which would cause me to lose any control much less make me ill. Too bad that I couldn't have had some marijuana during those years I entertained. I have no doubts that I would have been much more fun to be around.

My resolve, necessary to ward off the desire to have a little hit or two, has been fortified by my reaction to the viewing of the *Weeds* TV show. I watched the first three shows, and my disc still has two episodes on it. Should I watch those two shows? My Netflix plan requires that I return a DVD (I have Blu-Ray) before they will send me the next one. Therefore, I don't want to sit around for days deciding. I either watch it now or send it on its way back to Netflix with those two episodes unseen.

I read an article in today's paper that described a change in the classifications of the different forms of cocaine. Before the change, it was supposedly unfair in that young black men received much greater penalties than deserved. I can't give you the details because I am not familiar with them. Since many states have set up legislation for the utilization of medical marijuana outlets, the news of other pleasure drugs, such as ecstasy and even amphetamines, has decreased. Medical marijuana is a biggie now as I write these words. Why haven't I obtained a medical marijuana approval card? Well, one good reason is that I didn't apply. I have a condition, restless leg syndrome, which probably is on the list of conditions for which medical cards are available. My doctors have been generally conservative, and I never felt right about approaching them. I could have gone to one of the "strip mall" type MDs, which have a tiny storefront office, with the money ready to obtain their medical marijuana permit. I thought about it many times. Another reason for my hesitation was that I did not want to go on record as being a pot smoker. After all, it was still illegal federally, even though the state allowed these medical marijuana outlets.

The articles that I have read related to the various states that allow my drug of choice to be bought at medical marijuana facilities were exciting. It reminded me of the stories I heard while in Europe of the great variety of choices available in the government-sanctioned section of Amsterdam. I met a number of travelers who had been in Amsterdam, but fear of arrest kept them from carrying any of the goods with them when traveling to other countries. One couple told me they regretted that they didn't keep some to enjoy on the balance of their travels because they did not find any serious luggage inspections when traveling from country to country. But having pot in your possession when coming back to the USA was definitely a no-no. The same is true when traveling to Mexico. One friend of mine, seeing that the customs officers had a sniffing dog at the returning-to-the-states inspection area, was fortunate to have the opportunity to dump his contraband prior to his inspection.

DAY 47: BUYING SHIT

It is difficult for me to believe that this is the forty-seventh day with no weed. I am pleased and have found that, to this point, the removal of smoking grass as a sleep enhancer has been the most missed usage. Of course, the easing of tensions comes in number two as most missed, and the lightening of my seriousness is number three. The big question at the end of this diary is, shall I begin using again or should I continue my abstinence forever?

Upon finishing this diary/book and the activities related to having it published, I plan to begin writing another book. Now that may change if I establish some type of non-profit Web site to assist troubled users and/or collect data that will be useful to those interested parties in the medical and psychological fields.

I just found a site (through Google) that has the words of over one hundred addicts who have been in withdrawal from marijuana for twenty-four months or less. I am going to print all of the statements from these pot addicts and study them. I will write a consensus of my conclusions from this large group of people who have withdrawn or tried to end their marijuana connection. In glancing through them, I already noticed the word "sleep" appears quite often.

I was at the local post office today to mail this unfinished manuscript to a literary agent, hopefully *my* literary agent. I had, at the same time, mailed my submissions letter to the agency. I got there at the opening time of nine in the morning, hoping to be the first in line, getting out quickly. But of course, it didn't work that way. In line before me was a man with a cart full of boxes to be mailed. Oh no! Well, I really wasn't in a hurry so I spoke to the man, or he spoke to me while we were waiting. Turns out he was moving to—small world, guess where—a small town in Texas fourteen miles from the border. I asked him about the problems with drug gangs that I had read about near the border, and I had even mentioned such activity in my submissions letter. He told me that every other night he went to sleep hearing gunshots. I would have liked to have spent more time with him, but he was then busy with the postal attendant.

If some of those drug-gang shootings, kidnappings, and even killings occur in more and more Texas towns, the talk about legalization will intensify. It should. The thought that innocent people, including children, are dying is very frightening, besides being horrible.

I had written earlier of the many different people I dealt with in purchasing my pot. Usually the grass that I purchased was an ounce, which would last me for about a month. The number of months that I would make my connection with the same person varied. There were times when, for whatever reason, the shit was hard to find and I didn't have a good steady source. That meant dealing with non-dealers, generally addicts just like me, who were paying for their habit by being a middle person and doing some selling. I preferred someone closer to the original source of the stuff. They were true dealers and always had good marijuana on hand.

I only once had a dealing person carrying a gun, and I was frightened. It was one of those times when there wasn't any shit around, and some of those friends who would normally help me were also out and finding it difficult to make a connection. A female friend of mine, a non-user, knew of my difficulty and said she knew of a source in South Central LA. Now I wasn't exactly anxious to go to that area, a known and active gang area, carrying five hundred dollars and buying some pot. Because I felt uneasy and the young lady had already set this meeting up, I went accompanied by my young lady friend. After we knocked on the door of this small house, a young woman, probably in her thirties answered. She was wearing jeans and a blouse, and she wore glasses. My accompanying friend had called this lady and told her about the time that we would be there, so the lady answering the door was expecting us. She invited us in to the living room where we engaged in a little small talk, and then the lady left the room. When she came back, she was not alone. With her was another lady, tough looking but courteous. She was wearing a sweater, loosely hung in such a way that I couldn't help but notice that stuck in her belt was a pistol. The lady in jeans and blouse had a plastic bag filled with pot, which she handed to me. I looked at it and opened it to take a sniff. It was obvious to me that this was not five hundred dollars worth of buds but Mexican shit worth about seventy-five dollars. Now what?

I was thinking but only for a moment. I gave the lady my five hundred dollars in twenties, which she counted, while the lady with the pistol made some small talk with my friend. The count was good. I thanked them both and we left and quickly drove off, not stopping for anything. I wasn't alone in being surprised by the sight of the pistol. My friend apologized and said that she was just as scared as I was. That was my last trip in the direction of South Central LA.

DAY 48: WIKIPEDIA

Today is Sunday. We say that word, Sunday, without thinking. I am not saying that we think about the words Monday, Tuesday, etc. It's just that Sunday must have something to do with the sun. I don't think that "mon" or "tues" or "wed" or "thurs" or "fri" or even "sat" could or should initiate our thinking, but "sun" should. I am sure that some who read this journal will know something special about this day. Maybe someday I'll investigate. Sunday means the *Sunday Seattle Times* paper will be delivered. Everything is bigger, and maybe even better in Sunday's paper. The Jumble is seven words compared to five words the rest of the week. The crossword is huge on Sunday. The comics are in color. The commercial sections are glossy and heavy. The news section contains "Passages," a listing of special people who have passed during the week. Do people, as they get older, think about the possibility that they will be in "Passages" when they die? I do, although that is not a biggie for me. Want to know what is a biggie for me? It's being in the Sunday crossword. I'd like my name to be in the *New York Times Sunday* Crossword, but I'll take any crossword. Think that is too far out to desire? Well I think *Zilch* gives me a chance. I know it's a long shot, but what do I have to lose for it's only a dream. All this talk about the Sunday newspapers is happening because it arrives later in the morning. If it were here, this paper talk would never have been written. Why? Because I would be reading it!

What I am reading, in front of me now, is the Wikipedia (the free encyclopedia) about the effects of cannabis (accessed February 11, 2011). It reads, "Cannabis has both psychological and physiological effects on the human body." Continuing it reads, "Acute effects while under the influence can include **euphoria, anxiety, and short-term memory loss.**" It reads of concerns about the potential of long-term consumption (that's me) to increase risk for schizophrenia, bipolar disorders, and major depression, but all conclusions are disputed.

That paragraph is followed by a lengthy discussion of the cannabis chemistry, which is too complicated for me to tackle. The next statement is about me. It's entitled, "Sustainability in the body," quickly followed by the opener of the paragraph thusly, "Most cannabinoids are lipophilic (fat soluble) compounds that easily store in fat, thus yielding a long elimination half-life relative to other recreational drugs." That means even if you stop it is still in your body. And it states that drugs are recreational. It tells about the difficulty of overdosing, requiring one to smoke thousands of "joints" in a few minutes to kick the bucket, and even then, they are not positive that overdosing would occur. Next item. Short-term physical effects include increased heart rate, dry mouth (which I get often), reddening of the eyes (a dead giveaway for me), a reduction in intra-ocular pressure (helps prevent glaucoma?), muscle relaxation, and a sensation of cold or hot hands and feet (cold for me).

Next item. Psychoactive effects. Wait, let me break into this serious stuff for a moment. There are two types of risers in the morning, some call them owls and larks. Regardless of what you call them, it goes like this. One type, the lark, looks out the window and says, "Good morning, God." The other type, the owl, never even makes it to the window but says, "Good God, morning." This is one of many sayings that are comical but have some truth in them.

Back to psychoactive effects, known as a "high," which are totally subjective. They may include an altered state of consciousness, euphoria, feelings of well-being, relaxation or stress reduction, increased appreciation of humor, music or art, joviality, metacognition (what's that?) and introspection, enhanced recollection, increased sensuality, increased awareness of sensation, increased libido (hooray! hooray!), creative, abstract or philosophical thinking, disruption of linear memory, and paranoia or anxiety. NO WONDER IT'S HARD TO GIVE IT UP!! They go on. "Cannabis also produces many subjective and highly tangible effects, such as greater enjoyment of food taste and aroma" (munchies), and crazy about music and comedy. Another mentioned here is the subjective impression of long-elapsed time. This is one that I definitely was aware of, especially in the bedroom. I mentioned earlier, and probably will again, that the feeling of climax (the most pleasurable of all feelings, perhaps nature's way of insuring the propagation of the species) stretches a few seconds into what feels like minutes. The other bedroom subjective effect also (for men) involves the penis. It seems when I urinate, it is such a long period that I feel everybody about is thinking, "What the hell is Leo doing in there? He's been in there for ten minutes."

It closes out short-term effects with motor skills, reflexes, and attention affected, but it does not necessarily reflect impairment in terms of performance effectiveness, since few studies report increased accident risk (thank goodness). These are called neurological effects. Finally, it gives the long-term effects. That is me, so I will write for you the exact words in Wikipedia.

> Long-term effects of marijuana have not yet been fully studied due to federal government laws against marijuana research conducted by scientific method (verifying results of research independently and by multiple controlled sources).

I am willing to take tests to understand better the long-term effects. I would be very interested in taking the recent test related to the scan of the brain (after infused with a special fluid) in order to detect potential Alzheimer's problems or the latest eye test to detect material found in the brains of known Alzheimer's victims.

At the end of the site, it gives this very important comment, one of the prime reasons for disassociating marijuana from group one drugs.

Constraints on open research

> In many countries, experimental science regarding cannabis is restricted due to its illegality. Thus, cannabis as a drug is often hard to fit into the structural

confines of medical research because appropriate research-grade samples are difficult to obtain for research purposes, unless granted under authority of national governments.

Which gives stories like mine, when tied in with other long-term input, a place in studying marijuana until legal tests are conducted.

DAY 49: CONFIDENCE

I am not feeling a strong urge for a hit today. It's probably because I am not stressed. I have made peace with myself related to the submission I made to the literary agency. I have used a similar technique that I utilized many years ago when I was sales manager of Technology Instrument Corporation. I remember this incident clearly because it became the groundwork for future stressful activities of this kind.

We, the company, had been very interested securing the order for a large quantity potentiometer package that Motorola in Chicago was about to make. Our company was located in Newbury Park, California. I telephoned Motorola and set up an appointment with the head purchasing manager for the next day. I had made reservations to fly and arrive in Chicago the next morning. This gave me very little time to prepare for this meeting. I checked in at a motel, showered, shaved, and dressed for the big and important meeting. I was starting to feel the pressure. We needed that order, and after discussions with our management, I knew exactly how much I had to play with for this potential big order.

As I was driving the rental car to the Motorola plant, I talked to myself. I had to approach this gentleman with confidence. The bid that I carried with me was a price that would enable us to do well with a contract of this magnitude. I did have an okay to reduce the price if required for not losing the order, but that would have made it a borderline profitable contract. This type of contract was always difficult. You want it and need it, but you don't like to take it at a price that could turn disastrous if anything went wrong. I know this may sound simple to you, but I repeated to myself over and over, *Leo, you are not going to lose an arm or a leg. The worst thing that can happen to you is that you lose the order. You will not be injured in any way, so be happy and confident. Your confidence will be sensed by the purchasing chief, and you will get the order at the good price.* As I was greeted by the friendly and good-looking receptionist, I, too, was friendly. I was feeling good, my talk had strengthened my confidence, and it came out in my talk and in my walk. The meeting lasted less than twenty minutes. I didn't lose an arm or a leg! I got the order at the price that I knew the people back home would be extremely pleased. I left that Motorola plant feeling on top of the world and knowing that I would use this way of approaching critical situations in the future. Not just for sales orders but for any worrisome crisis like a job interview or during a negotiation for a salary increase or a higher position in a company.

I feel strongly that it would be much better to have a creditable and successful literary agent approaching book publishers on my behalf than to approach them myself. If I am unsuccessful with this literary agent, there are others. If I am unable to obtain a literary agent, then I must pursue publishers myself. If I am unable to click with any book publisher, then I will have to use a subsidy publisher. Through all of these efforts and trials, I will remember that time at Motorola. I will not lose an arm or a leg. I have a good book, and it will be published.

Today was the last day of the Senior Open for the Champion's Tour, the tour for players fifty and over. This is a special tournament because it is being played within twenty miles from where I reside. Unfortunately, I didn't go because I couldn't handle the walking. Depending on the distance from the parking lot to the golf course, I may not even be capable of making it to the course, much less try to walk around the course, which had a large-spectator day. The attendance was excellent because a hometown player, Fred Couples, grew up and played his first golf here. He was tied for the lead after the first three days, and everyone in the Seattle area was excited, including me. This information I am writing now comes after the tournament was over. There was no writing during the tournament today. You probably guessed that Fred Couples did not win for had he done so I would have written his name in caps and with a number of hoorays. An exciting *couple* of TV viewing hours watching *Couples*.

DAY 50: END DECISION

There are numerous questions that come to mind often during this withdrawal process. Why aren't I having a more difficult experience being without my pot? What happens when I reach the end of this diary?

I am not having a seriously difficult time not smoking my pot. I think it is partially because the pleasure that I get from getting loaded is not as joyous as it was years ago. I believe that as the years of usage pile up I am not as sensitive to the cannabinoids. I think that if I had a partner and we would smoke together I would enjoy it more. It has become almost a medication for me; the biggest application is to help me sleep.

Another reason I am not having a problem not smoking my pot is because I am somewhat of a control freak and I get very upset with myself when I decide to do something and then don't do it. The withdrawal has not given me any pain or discomfort except for the yearning, but since I haven't been overly nervous, I can control my itch.

The big question will come at the completion of this diary. Will I have very good pleasures if I smoke it on a limited scale? I mean, let's say, twice a week. Could I control my intake on that type of schedule? I sit here, writing about my withdrawal, but now I am also writing and thinking about my using, albeit at a lesser scale, at the end of this diary. Right now I feel good without my grass, but I still have that yearning to feel better. I believe that if marijuana is legalized and we have more testing results, I would feel better about using again.

I hope that I will learn a lot from others who are long-term addicts and respond to my invitations.

I am sitting here in this early morning, trying to think of people who smoked pot as much as I did. The only person that comes to mind is Jim, my golfing friend during my last years of playing. We played together in the Seniors' Club at El Cariso. We had a group of players, anywhere from four to fifteen, who played together twice a week. Two or three members of that group were starters, people who work behind the counter, taking your money and giving you an assigned starting time. El Cariso was a county course with the lowest golf fees of any course that I played. The men that I played with were retired working men, who loved the game as much as I. It was in those last six or seven years of playing that I smoked grass on the course, usually with Jim, who was one of my friends who smoked as much as I did. He also smoked cigarettes, and I had an arrangement with him. I would "bum" a cigarette or two or three during the eighteen holes we played together. Then I would get one or two to smoke after our round was finished, and then all of us that played that day would gather in the clubhouse. Now this was not a very fancy clubhouse. It had an outside balcony where our gang would sit and talk. But the prime activity was to drink beers. I was not a drinker so I would enjoy my casual smokes with juice or a diet soda. Jim only smoked the cheapest of the cheap brand filtered cigs. People used to tease me about bumming cigarettes. They said I only smoked "OPs," which stood for "Other People's." What they didn't know was that I frequently bought a pack of the variety that Jim liked and gave them to him. The others didn't know of these transactions, and I am sure they thought of me as a cheapskate, but to be honest, this arrangement cost me more than if I had bought the cigs for myself.

After my wife, Barbara, left (we got married after being together for six years), I didn't have anyone that I smoked my grass with on any kind of regular basis. My sister didn't smoke. She lived in Fallbrook about 120 miles from my place, but her son Gary did. He was usually at the house when I visited, and we did smoke together. He usually had some good stuff, and I would always bring some of the best that I had. We enjoyed our smoke together, but it wasn't like the early days with Barbara and some of our smoking friends. My children did not smoke grass until they were in their thirties, or so I thought. I later found out that my oldest son smoked shit probably starting in his late teens after he was on his own.

DAY 51: WIFE OF MY LIFE

DON'T BE SAD, BE GLAD FOR WHAT YOU HAD!
I have come up with a small number of little words that combined are huge. My "WHAT ARE WE" series is on the opening page of my Website and fits that category but in a different environment than:
DON'T BE SAD, BE GLAD FOR WHAT YOU HAD!

I can apply it to the circumstances in which I find myself at the present time. I am giving up a joy. I had the pleasures of marijuana for forty years, and as you can tell from the writings of the first fifty days, it has been good for me and has not made me pay any penalties during this withdrawal period. But this expression has helped me much more significantly in the past. This expression has given me a state of peace and appreciation and a happy and content base for the balance of my time on this planet Earth. In order to reveal to you the source of this phrase, I will have to devote a few days of this diary to the story.

This story is about the happiest times of my life. This story is about a selfish controlling man who was in love with the most wonderful person he has ever met and known. This story is about a person, the most unselfish being I have ever met. This story is about a caring person, who—I find myself searching for a word that doesn't exist—who was sinless. The story starts in Fort Lauderdale, Florida, in the year 1969.

I had started a manufacturer's representative business with a partner. We had lined up clients whose products we had fair knowledge of, and I was to cover the Ft. Lauderdale and Miami area while my partner was based in Orlando, covering the middle of the state. One of my customers was Oster Manufacturing, and I had met with their engineering personnel a number of times. It seems to me that I had previous experiences with Oster at another plant in another state, but I am not sure.

One late afternoon, while I was finishing up my workday at my apartment, I received a phone call from a member of the Oster engineering staff. He was troubled as he was going through a divorce, and he knew that I was a veteran of the divorce wars. He wanted to get together and pick my brain or just talk about his feelings. So there was a bar very close to my apartment that he was familiar with, and we decided to meet there within the hour. Once there, we talked and drank and drank and talked. I was drinking my Compari tall with lime, with which I could go on for hours. His drinks were a little stronger. There was a jukebox in this bar, which was nearly empty except for two attractive young ladies also sitting at the bar. The more intoxicated my Oster engineer became, the more I became interested in the two ladies at the bar. I'll make a long story short by telling you that I left that bar with one of the young ladies whose name was Barbara. We went to a well-known cocktail lounge and spent a few hours getting to know each other. We even got to know each other better at my apartment early the next morning.

Within a day or two, we had dinner together at a beautiful classy restaurant called the something Winder, I can't think of the exact name. But I remember the craziest little item that evening. It was that I was wearing Patchouli. Why I remember that, I don't know. The next day I picked her up, and she joined me at the golf course, which allowed her to ride with me in a cart and not play. Not all courses allowed that. We had a fun time, and not that it made any difference but Jackie Gleason was playing in a foursome a few holes ahead of us.

Within in a week, she moved in with me. She was working as a secretary for an insurance company; Colonial Penn, I believe was the name. I lived very near the inland waterway, and on this water was a cocktail lounge called the Bunny something, which had a live band and a dance floor. Well, I loved to dance, and it turns out that she was the best dance partner I ever had. She was about 112 pounds and five feet four inches tall. A perfect fit. She had blond hair and a gorgeous figure with a lovely smile on a very symmetrical face. This lady, Barbara, was hot. We danced the night away a few times at that lounge. I have in my possession an album that was recorded in that lounge. We were not there for the recording, and I did not know about this recording until many, many years later.

Things were not going that well in the rep business so I was looking for another job. I had an offer to become a sales manager for a plastic potentiometer company in the northeast, Massachusetts. I also had an offer to be a marketing manager for an audio-video business in Hollywood, California. The latter came from an old co-worker of mine, and he had obtained an option to buy the business if we could turn it around. So I accepted that one. I had a rental car, and Barbara and I packed it with as much as we could, and we had a trailer that carried the majority of our stuff. We headed north and stopped in Orlando to see my partner. I found out that I could not take the rental car out of the state. Big trouble. I was low on funds, and this was going to be a credit-card trip. Barbara had a Toyota back at her mother's place in Ft. Lauderdale, and she was willing to fly from Orlando to Fort L. and get her car. We would cross the country in her little Toyota. Remember, at that time, the Japanese cars were small and cheap; they were just getting started in the USA. We found a moving company that would transport our cart of household goods. So off we went. We made it across country with very few stops because we both drove. At the time, the movie *Butch Cassidy and the Sundance Kid* was hot. In it was a song called "Raindrops Keep Falling on My Head," and all the way across this land of ours, Barbara tried to teach me the lyrics of that song. I never learned them, but that's another story.

Barbara was only twenty and somewhat of a shy person with limited confidence in herself. I recognized this trait and was determined to help her become more confident. She was sharp, the best female wit I ever met. She was very attractive. She was a fantastic typist and hard worker. There was absolutely no basis for her lack of confidence.

During the fifteen years that we were together, I was a very, very poor provider. I haven't described our living situation during those years, but I will now. First habitat after arriving from Florida was on Hollywood Boulevard in a furnished apartment with a pool. We were on the second floor, facing Hollywood Boulevard. What was I thinking? Dummy me. Well the rent was reasonable, and I had a salary at Magnetic TVI (located across the street from Pink's), which was at the intersection of La Brea and Melrose, two busy and well-known thoroughfares in Hollywood. I could and did walk there from our apartment although we did have Barbara's Toyota parked in the underground parking lot of the apartment. We started looking for a job for Barbara (I never called her Barb) and were able to set up some interviews. These did not result in any offers, so Barbara told me, but later I found out that she never went to the interviews. After I learned of this behavior, we had long discussions about our needs and her abilities, and things changed rapidly. She got a very good job with some union, and it was in Hollywood on Barham, not more than a mile from our place.

So we were there only about two weeks, and things looked good until … One morning Barbara went down to the garage, and the Toyota was gone. Oh no! What next? Well we immediately called the police and told them our car had been stolen. They came to obtain the details. Among the early questions they asked was, "Was it a repo?" I told them no, it was a Toyota. I was thirty-five years old but did not know that term "repo" meant repossessed. How could that be? I had just sent two payments, and we had equity in the car. I was really angry, but it didn't matter. Apparently there was some clause in the contract that stipulated no taking the car out of the state of Florida. So we found ourselves with no money to speak of and no car. Although I didn't know it, this was a portent of the economic conditions of our whole time together. I told you earlier that I was a very, very poor provider during our relationship although I was always an optimist and never at that early stage of our togetherness could have predicted the financially lacking years ahead. So needing some wheels immediately, I walked down La Brea about four or five blocks past Magnetic TVI, my place of employment, to the automobile row of La Brea and found, in the back rows of the used car lots, an old Dodge that had a selling price of $189.00. I bought it with my credit card and drove it home. I don't remember the actual model year of the car, but you can guess from the price that it was old. But it ran and would get Barbara to her job and get us around the city.

After about a year and a half, my friend and boss, Harry, told me the option period had run out and the owner, Cap Kieruff, had come back to take over. Well, at least we had turned the operation around, mainly from the pilferage protection video rental systems I had established. This was a great source of income once we had installed the equipment, primarily consisting of video cameras (both real and dummies) and CRT monitors. Of course, we had the expense of installation, but we offered that service to the clients at no charge. So a potential customer could have this protection from theft with no initial cost, just a rental fee. The cost of the cameras and monitors was very reasonable, and in just six months rental time, our initial equipment and installation costs were recovered. From then on, it was gravy. So when Harry left, he was able to take the pilferage business with him. I believe he later added some neighborhood washer/dryer businesses and was doing well.

In the meantime, he introduced me to a gentleman who was in the electro-polishing business and machine shop business in the San Fernando Valley, just over the hill from where Barbara and I lived. It was not a high-paying job, and it had poor long-term possibilities. But I had to get work soon, and this looked like a highly exotic and exciting project involving something that had never been accomplished before in the world. What was it? It was the electro-polishing of the interior surfaces of tubing. I am not going to attempt to go into the details except to tell you that the initial project involved one-hundred-foot-long metal tubing eventually to be used in a salt-water conversion project. Interesting that when I attempt to obtain any information related to this project (worked on in pre-Internet years), even though the venture company involved was Ford Aeroneutronics, I find nothing of it on the Web of today.

Barbara had changed jobs, and her income was very significant in our daily lives, for over the next six or seven years, I never made a good salary for any length of time. How bad was it? It was a month-to-month existence, but we were in love, enjoyed our togetherness, smoked our pot, and even had some dogs, which Barbara especially enjoyed. I loved that lady. She never complained during any of our financial difficulties. She was absolutely wonderful. We eventually could not afford a small rent increase of the small and isolated house we lived in for about two years. We were fortunate in that our landlord, who lived in Whitley Heights, introduced us to a couple who lived and owned one of the large homes built around the turn of the century. We had the majority of the upstairs area, small, but at a rent of one hundred dollars a month, we would have lived in a doghouse at that time. And this location gave us a magnificent view of the city below us, and on especially clear days of the year (maybe ten), we could actually see the Pacific Ocean in Santa Monica and also the bridge at Long Beach.

Our financial situation worsened because we were in the midst of a recession and I was not finding a job. Barbara and I began an ultra conservative expenditure control plan. I obtained those large lined accounting sheets, and we recorded every penny that we spent. Not for a month, not for a year, but for years. Any other woman would, after about eight years of this type of living situation, have said adios. After all, she had a decent income, she was gorgeous, and men pursued her on the job and everywhere else too. But no complaints.

During this difficult economic time, I felt the need to begin a new career in a field, which I felt and knew was growing rapidly. I always knew that one would have a greater opportunity to improve himself in a growing market, and this market, COMPUTERS, I knew was going to be a good one. I also felt that it was right up my alley for I already had been looking into the first home type computers of that time, some of which were kits. Also, I had written software specifications in 1971 when I was at Chronometrics. So with Barbara's blessing, I entered into a school called Computer Learning Center for a full-time, six-month training period. I loved it and excelled even though I was forty-six years of age and most of my fellow students were in their twenties. I won't take your time outlining the computer languages and other education presented in this learning program. But I will say that I worked every evening, doing either homework or preparing for the next day's learning activities. I had never worked so diligently in any other of my educational endeavors. I graduated with all As and eventually obtained a position with the Los Angeles school system. It wasn't easy either. I had attended an employment test examination offered by the city of Burbank for computer positions in the city's computer programming operations. Over fifty people participated in this four-hour marathon test for what I thought was multiple positions but later found out that there was only one opening. I came in second after all the test results had been announced—no job offer for me. Much later, I learned that they already had a prime candidate for this position, and so it goes. However, at this time, the Los Angeles school district was in need of computer programming personnel, and they offered interviews to the top five candidates of the Burbank test. I interviewed and got the job at the LA schools. It was sort of a conditional type of position with no benefits and a six-month trial period. I will not take any more of your time going on my growth in both position and pay at the district. The important point is that for the first time in our relationship, Barbara had a partner who was bringing in a steady and gradually growing salary.

So one reading this diary would surmise a bright future ahead for the two lovers after having weathered difficult financial problems during their ten years together. But I haven't made mention of two personal happenings that eventually caused our marriage and fifteen-year relationship to end. When we originally got together, our sexual relations were terrific, and Barbara and I both enjoyed our bedtime together. I had wondered if this great fun would be affected in a negative way in the future. What I mean is that when we got together, I, at age thirty-seven, was at my sexual peak and Barbara, at age twenty, would probably reach her sexual peak at age thirty-five. Well my worst nightmare became real. I had never heard of the term, erectile dysfunction, but as I got to my late forties, I had problems. At the time, I didn't understand, but I knew there was something wrong. I could achieve a nice erection, but before I could act upon it, it was gone. Now this didn't happen overnight, but there were failures from time to time. For quite a while, I thought it may have been caused by the reduced level of excitement for me, not Barbara, which might have been due to our many years together. So I found myself fooling around. My explorations had nothing to do with love, but I thought maybe some new and fresh sexual successes would solve my erection problem. Never did. I had the same problem, even worse because of the guilt I felt in these extra-marital forays.

Eventually, Barbara was affected, I believe, by the waning sexual pleasures of our relationship, and I hadn't helped things, possibly, because I didn't know what was going on. The worst possible outcome of this situation, at least as far as I was concerned, was happening. We started to receive hang-up phone calls, and Barbara began to come home from work at a later time quite often. We had little or no sex at all. I knew she was having an affair. I knew in my heart that something was going on. But I never asked her about it. I never followed her in an attempt to discover what and who was she involved with. It was extremely difficult, but I had made up my mind that I would wait for her to tell me what was happening. I went through a horrible period, knowing that the woman that I dearly loved and I had felt would be my partner for life was cheating on me. Somehow, I felt that the years of closeness that we had and the wonderful person that she was would have her confess to what was happening. She did, but it was probably months after the affair had begun, and to me, it was years. It was on my mind constantly. We tried counseling, but it was over for us. I still had my erectile dysfunction problem, and it wasn't long before she moved out. I was heartbroken but didn't know what to do.

It turns out that it became more complicated because the other man was married with children. So Barbara moved out and then back, but not for long. Apparently, they had worked things out. Not long after, they moved to the East Coast, but Barbara and I kept in contact. I wanted her to be my friend forever. It was I who obtained a divorce. Although I missed her terribly, I still wanted her to be happy and maybe even enjoy the goodies in her life that I never had provided. Her new partner was capable of producing a good income, for his work was usually at a high level of management positions.

For the next ten years, I suffered the consequences of my inability to achieve and maintain an erection. I had very few dates over those years, and I devoted my time to serious studies of my interest in human behavior, which was now compounded by my sexual failings. Every day after work, I would hit the grass and the books, starting with primarily books related to psychology. In addition, I read everything I found in the newspaper or magazines and eventually on the Web that could shed light on my erection problems. I was collecting many books, mostly purchased at extremely reasonable prices from Edward R. Hamilton Bookseller. My reading had progressed to the extent that I finally had grasped the theories of Freud. This learning opened up many doors of understanding for me that next got me into the study of evolution and Darwin's theories. I must say that this new learning was very exciting for me and offset many days and months that could have been seriously depressing. As I became more and more knowledgeable with the fields of psychology and evolution, I found myself purchasing books of philosophy. I had turned into a virtual scholar.

My continual searches for any material related to my erectile dysfunction problem resulted in some hopeful information. An article in one of my journals that I was subscribing to had an address of a doctor in the Seattle area that had some excellent results with the injection of a chemical called papaverine into the penis. I wrote to this doctor and received a response directing me to a urologist in Santa Monica. I made an appointment, and after proper examinations and my signing declarations freeing the doc from disastrous results, I had my first injection in his office. I wound up with the strongest erection of the past twelve years. I drove home on Wilshire Boulevard, about twelve miles to my home in Hollywood with an erection that caused me to pray not to have an accident or a ticket situation. That rock of hard-on lasted beyond the trip home, at least three-quarters of an hour in total.

How exciting for me. But this was just the beginning of the efforts needed to utilize this new technique. I felt like a pioneer, which I really was. Remember this is pre-Viagra time. Now I had possibilities but no partner. And the status of the application of the magical substance required a trip to the urologist to obtain the syringe containing the solution. The working life of the solution was short, a couple of days as I remember. So at first having no, pardon the expression, guinea pig to try out my new found pecker hardness, I experimented with masturbation.

Eventually I started dating, but then there were other problems. For one, the injection procedure was not that simple. It had to be done correctly, or painful conditions occurred. Plus timing was a problem that had to be overcome. It didn't work very well to attempt romancing the potential sex partner to the point of warmth and then excuse myself while I went to the closed-door bathroom to inject. Sometimes the concoction was too old and didn't work, and sometimes I injected improperly giving pain instead of pleasure.

Eventually with the assistance of a lovely and understanding young lady to whom I am grateful to this very day, and remain friends with, I achieved the sexual pleasures for me and my partner that I had dreamed about for years. The next step in the application was obtaining the chemicals in a kit. No more trips to the urologist. Just mix the chemicals, insert them into a syringe, inject, and—oolah—within five minutes, a good strong erection. But this was still not the final application technique. Reminds me of the CD in music audio being promoted as the ultimate in the presentation of music to the listener, but wait ... here comes the digital world of MP3s. The final and still the best way for those who do not react favorably with the pill-medicated Viagra or Cialis or any of the others, like me who tried them all, is to read carefully the next few sentences to obtain erections resembling those of your youth. But remember your desire must be powerful to accept the idea of the injection of a needle into your penis, a concept too frightening for many men.

Here, right here on this page, I am imparting to you the knowledge that will enable you not just to please but to totally excite and arouse your sexual partner. First, the latest and simplest—filling the syringe. The compound required now can be obtained at many pharmacies in a vial that has a shelf life of a year or more. The syringes can also be purchased at any pharmacy, but be sure to obtain the short-needle version. The area to receive the compound is that soft tissue that fills up with blood, resulting in the erection.

The cream on the cake for me was the placement of a cock ring pushed as close to the base of the penis as possible, making it very unlikely that the blood will flow from the penis back into your body and thereby weakening the erection.

I want to close this long and extensive segment of my diary with another of my phrases of a few short words that has been helpful to me and maybe will be for you.

NOTHING IS FOREVER EXCEPT DEATH.

So whether it is pain or pleasure, these few words are applicable.

NOTHING IS FOREVER EXCEPT DEATH.

DAY 52: THE CHURCH

Feeling good this morning. I am hungry so I have cut up a peach and a banana, put them on a plate; making some decaf coffee, and will enjoy all in a short time after the *Seattle Times* arrives. While I was in my bed before rising, I thought about what I would enter in my diary today. As I had stated earlier, most people who keep diaries write in them in the evening, before retiring. It gives them the opportunity to discuss and go over the day's happenings. I feel tired before I retire, and I doubt that I would be able to write something on a regular basis. But no matter how few hours I sleep, I seem to have much more energy to complete this task upon rising. After all, I am a lark, looking out the window and saying, "Good morning, God." And that brings me to the topic of today's entry, the Church.

Freud said that for many, religion brings order out of chaos. I am a Lutheran by my early church activities, not my choice but the choice of my father who never attended church. I was baptized and confirmed in a Lutheran church where the main Sunday services were in German. I attended catechism class for three years, one day a week the first year, two days the second year, and three days the third year. I will have to check with my sister to verify this schedule because I don't remember. Apparently, we were taught from the Lutheran's small catechism, which was written by Martin Luther in the year 1529. This catechism contains the Apostles' Creed, the Lord's Prayer, the Sacrament of the Holy Baptism, the Office of the Keys and Confession, and the Sacrament to the Eucharist. Unfortunately, or maybe fortunately, I do not remember any of this except that our task was to memorize this book.

Today, as I write this diary, I am a non-believer in organized religion and a non-believer that a God exists. Why this young man, who was what I call brainwashed in the beliefs of the Lutheran faith as written in Luther's Catechism, became a non-believer is related to the knowledge of the history of the human race that I acquired. It was further pronounced by the very visible hypocrisy practiced by the parishioners of my church and other members of all kinds of organized religions.

DAY 53: WHY GOD?

The human species, before language, was thought to live in caves and, I feel, must have existed very much like chimps or other close relatives. I would imagine that humans then had a very short life span and that the females were often pregnant, starting at a very young age. They had established crude communication abilities that were required to work as a unit in order to slay other creatures for food.

As they grew in numbers, they began to build shelters and lived in small villages. Eventually, they required some rules that would enable them to live together without major conflict within the tribe. These rules would have been established by the elders of the tribe who needed to find methods to have the tribe's people obey them. The humans at that time could be seriously frightened by thunder and lightning. The elders sensed this fear and believed that they could use these natural activities to induce the tribe members to obey the rules. If they did not, then the gods of the sky, thunder and lightning, would punish them. This method of policing was very practical and apparently worked well for many years.

But there were problems with this method of maintaining some type of order among the tribe's people. For one thing, the thunder at times was very sporadic and did not occur for long periods of time. And the elders couldn't call for thunder to punish a rule breaker, and the tribal chiefs couldn't always be there when these disorderly events occurred. The chieftains needed a method for keeping constant surveillance over the wild members of their tribe. This is where and how some form of organized religion began. A god above all gods was omnipresent, and the chieftains chose members who were said to have a relationship and could communicate with this great god. Regular gatherings were conducted to inform the tribe members of the god's wishes and desires, thus inducing tribe's people to worship and obey. Sometimes such actions as sacrifices were used to strengthen the power of the god and cause much fear in the tribe's people.

As time went forward, this religious contingent of the tribe grew in numbers and power. Language was growing in use among the tribes, and the religious group was well suited to sophisticate their overall religious ways since they did not have other responsibilities such as hunting, fishing, and fighting.

Then as the humans started moving about the earth, many of the powerful religious gained even more authority, having special temples and rich clothing to strengthen further their control. And as the use of language became more sophisticated, the religious leaders organized their teachings and recruited members outside of the main tribe.

From these crude beginnings, eventually, a few strong religions were created, and hierarchies were established, and missionaries traveled the world to recruit and convert others to participate in their religion.

DAY 54: MEDICATION TRIAL

Last night was the first night in over ten years that I did not take my Mirapex medication for my restless leg syndrome. I will not take any Mirapex today and tonight. If I can get through that period of time without feeling the symptoms of RLS, it will be a major breakthrough. In all of the studies that I have read on the Web, none indicated a relationship between marijuana and RLS. I hope I am not premature, but we will soon see.

Sorry for me. I was fine until about noon, and then all hell broke loose. My RLS came alive with fervor, and I was forced to medicate. However, now it is at ten at night, and I feel OK. Question is should I take a pill now or go to bed and see what happens? I will try without.

This evening my daughter was visiting from Portland, and I had the opportunity to be with the family when they were high and I wasn't. Not good. It has been so long since I have been totally free of marijuana as I am right now and in the company of those that are loaded. I really felt out of place, and again, the seriousness of my general mood does not fit with the others when they are high. It comes down to get loaded and fit in or else don't get loaded and stay away. The big question is, "Can a sober person be in a party of loaded people and enjoy the humor and antics of a loaded group?" I don't think I can. With heavy drinking or smoking, I would rather be absent.

DAYS 55-57: NO NEWS. NO THOUGHTS. ALL WRITTEN OUT. FEELING ANXIOUS!

DAY 58: TEST RUN

I find my demeanor to be nasty and short of patience lately. It seems that I enter that world of selfishness with my time. It is to be used for my projects and pleasures above all other potential requisitions for it. I have been neglecting Tweeter, my parakeet, and I am all he has for company. He needs a certain amount of attention; in fact he seems to beg for it. The time I spent with my children, son and daughter-in-law and daughter, was as pleasant as it should have been. They all had a hit or two, and I did not, of course. I found myself out of place as the day went on. I did a poor job of keeping up with and enjoying the "funnies" each participant tossed about; laughing was the norm.

These two incidents made me decide to make a test run by having a few hits and being aware of the behavior following and sensing the "high" that I expected. I was in the process of preparing a DVD for a friend but not doing very well. Twice in the slow process of burning the DVD, it aborted at 98 percent completion. I didn't know why, and today I still don't. My anger at this problem, added to the previous afternoon's difficulties, was the impetus for the test.

One other action possibly related to my withdrawal and hopefully very low amount of marijuana in my body was my blood pressure. The day before the test, my pressure was a marvelous reading of 127/61 on first read, 123/59 on the second read. I was very, very pleased with those measurements. What was the measurement after the test? I was pleased with that reading also; it was 131/59. These blood pressure measurements cannot tell me much about the smoking/non-smoking differences in one test run. However, all readings were very positive, somewhat eliminating any withdrawal changes based on blood pressure and achieved by my steady exercise program.

This one-day test run is significant if I can continue my withdrawal until I decide to make another test run or two. I am leaning to becoming a user again if I feel better about the Alzheimer's possibilities and I don't learn of any lung, throat, or phlegm negative symptoms. We shall see.

DAY 59: ALMOST THERE.

DAY 60: FINAL ANALYSIS

OBSERVATIONS

1. No physical discomfort and no withdrawal symptoms.
2. Munchies exist with or without marijuana.
3. Demeanor improves and social attitude lightens with marijuana.
4. No measurable change in memory and puzzle solving.
5. Improved patience with marijuana.
6. Exercise steady with or without marijuana.
7. Sleep is much better with marijuana.
8. RLS is less intensive with marijuana.
9. Stress is reduced with marijuana.
10. Blood pressure good before/after withdrawal.

CONCLUSION

On the basis of the above observations, I will continue with the use of marijuana, with the reservation that usage be reasonable and I be on the alert for lung and throat conditions.

ADDENDUM: MEDICAL MARIJUANA

I am a resident of the state of Washington and have been for four years. As I stated previously, I have had a good source for marijuana, but that source has dried up. I decided that I have been using my marijuana mostly to aid in sleeping and to relieve my RLS (restless leg syndrome). So I began an effort to find a medical marijuana provider that was geographically close and in a somewhat conservative safe area.

Of course, I was nervous about going this route for it would announce my pot usage to the world. But what the hell do I think this book will do? I guess that is the main force that enabled me to suppress my worries about going legal.

Everybody knows or will know soon!

So I started by getting a list of all of the medical marijuana offices in the Seattle/Lynnwood area, using Google, of course. It listed the medical marijuana dispensaries in or near Lynnwood. On top of the list was Satica Medical Group, located on Firdale Avenue within five miles of my residence. I liked their name, which is a combo of sativa and indica, the two most popular of the marijuana plants offered.

I placed a call to Satica and spoke to their representative about my desire to enroll in the Washington State Medical Marijuana plan. He informed me of the various criteria for obtaining a permit to purchase from the medical marijuana dispensers. I emailed copies of my prescriptions related to my problems with RLS. Apparently, the Satica has a medical doctor who reviews all of their potential patients seeking approval. Within forty-eight hours, I received an email from

Satica, notifying me that permission was okayed and I should come to their office to complete all of the activities and answer any other questions related to my approval. I paid the Satica group $150 to cover the cost for the work of the doctor issuing the permit.

Two days later, I paid a visit to the facility of Satica. I was somewhat concerned that their staff was very young, but they probably knew much more about marijuana than I knew even though I had smoked grass for over forty years. They proceeded to give me a lecture on the various limitations and requirements of the Washington State law related to medical marijuana. Unfortunately or maybe fortunately, I had seen the facilities and wares of various medical marijuana dispensaries in the USA on television. The Satica outfit did not compare with any of the displays that I had seen. They had a very small office, which was not very attractive, and very few items on display. They only had three or four types of marijuana available.

I was not familiar with the various "titled" pot types such as Haze, Super Skunk, Purple Haze, etc. Since I was not very knowledgeable about these choices presented to me, I planned to purchase small quantities of various types to evaluate them. I purchased ten dollars each of three different individual pot types. These were really small amounts, one gram each, for a total cost of thirty dollars. My plan was to test these three bags and attempt to pick the best of the trio. Sounds pretty simple, you think. Well, if you're a pot smoker, you very well know that smoking the same pot at different times doesn't always produce the same feelings. There are many factors affecting the high given by smoking marijuana, but the major factor is the grass itself. But the smoker's mood, his pre-smoke diet, the pressures of daily work, present company if any, the paraphernalia utilized, and on and on. It's a wonder the drug is so popular when its performance falters sometimes too often.

So I purchased my test bags and said good day to the staff of Satica. I was pleased that my whole introductory experience into the medical marijuana of the state of Washington was a good one. I had some extended discussions of the state's marijuana law with the staff that gave me the feeling that these people realize the importance of adhering to the requirements of the law. And they invested time in helping me understand them.

This is the first time in years and years that I had the opportunity to try different grass. It reminded me of a movie with Frank Sinatra. In this movie, he played a dope addict, and he was trying to withdraw. Well, his supplier didn't like the thought of losing a good customer. The seller told a story about a person who was hooked on candy. In order to quit, he told Sinatra that the candy person went to a large candy store and chose many varieties and such a large quantity that he was more than "candied" out. So then, this seller tried to convince Sinatra to visit the "dope" store and fill his need to the nth degree.

The point of this story is that I felt a rush when addressing the thought that I will be able to try all kinds of marijuana, but not at Satica. I knew I had to investigate and try to find a more sophisticated medical marijuana clinic similar to what I had seen on television. So I found another clinic within ten miles. I called them to get directions, which they gave to me, and I asked if there were anything that I should know about their clinic. The name of this clinic was the Green Hope Patient Network. I drove there, and after a small struggle, I found their offices in a small mall. Immediately, I felt the difference in this clinic from the Satica clinic that was my first choice. They told me that there would be a forty-dollar membership fee. I didn't understand why I should have to pay a fee, but they were adamant. I couldn't even enter the clinic's room devoted to their stock in marijuana and various tasty looking cookies and cakes. So I paid the fee!

Oh my goodness! It was like the candy store. A square tray about two feet by two feet had sixteen squares, each filled with a bag of marijuana. Each bag was identified, and the buyer (me) had the opportunity to open the bag and smell and study the pot. I was not aware of any rule which stated that you could or could not sample (smoke) any marijuana. I did not want to have any hits while I was at the clinic, so I never bothered to ask for permission. I still don't know.

Somewhere I had read or heard about a very popular marijuana named White Widow. Before I had entered this clinic, I was hoping that they would have White Widow and some of the others that I have read about. Let me list a few of the hundred or more marijuana strains supposedly available somewhere: Mauwie Wauwie, Afghani, California Skunk, Natural Buds, Medijuana, Strawberry Ice, Skunk

Red Hair, Skunk Weed, Skunk Special (lots of skunks). The basic cannabis families are named Sativa and Indica.

Although this addict has been addicted for over forty years, I don't know much about the marijuana growing regimens or the seed varieties that are used. Let's face it; if you were a pot user in the past forty years, you didn't announce it to the world. I have golfing friends that I have known and played golf with for over thirty years. One friend, Jim, has been a grass smoker for many years. I did not know that! We had played golf together in the same foursome for at least eight years, both being potheads but unknown to either of us. You realize that a round of golf consumes about five hours of non-grass smoking time. And then, that "no smoking" changed for Jim and me, but the five hours stayed the same. One ordinary day on the golf course with my regular foursome, including Jim, became an extraordinary day. I called it REVELATION DAY. It was on this day during this round of golf that we found each other out. Jim knew I was a user, and I knew that he was a user. How that happened on that day, I don't remember, but it was important because it opened the door for further revelations from other golf buddies of mine.

None of my newfound smokers has ever mentioned problems from marijuana. The complaints that I usually heard were related to the difficulty in obtaining good stuff.

Some users presently get their shit from a dealer even though they have a medical problem that could result in an okay for a license, but they have chosen not to go that route. These "using" friends were frightened that the federal laws prohibiting all uses of marijuana could cause them problems. I am the first person that I know who has a medical marijuana license. Am I worried? Yes, I am, but I believe that these medical marijuana clinics are the beginning of the end of marijuana prohibition.

The purpose and intent of the Washington State Medical Marijuana law is to provide relief for some patients with terminal or debilitating illnesses for which marijuana appears to be beneficial, including chemotherapy-related nasclerosis and other spasticity disorders, epilepsy, acute or general glaucoma, and others. The Washington State Medical Marijuana law is #69.521A.010.

What are the criteria for designating a drug to be unlawful? Why is marijuana an illegal drug and alcohol legal? These are the questions that were active often during the writing of this book. There are many of us, users and non-users, who believe the government should not be controlling the usage of any drugs unless the user consistently causes harm to others. The accomplishment of free usage of marijuana, reducing present costly prohibition activities, will provide funds to concentrate our laws and police on those active users of troublesome drugs.